John Hart

So you think you're attracted to the same sex?

Penguin Books

Penguin Books Ltd, Harmondsworth, Middlesex, England
Penguin Books, 40 West 23rd Street, New York, New York 10010, U.S.A.
Penguin Books Australia Ltd, Ringwood, Victoria, Australia
Penguin Books Canada Ltd, 2801 John Street, Markham, Ontario, Canada L3R 1B4
Penguin Books (N.Z.) Ltd, 182–190 Wairau Road, Auckland 10, New Zealand

First published 1984

Made and printed in Great Britain by
Richard Clay (The Chaucer Press) Ltd, Bungay, Suffolk
Filmset in 10 on 11½ pt Monophoto Sabon by Northumberland Press Ltd, Gateshead

Penguin Books

So you think you're attracted to the same sex?

Born in London in 1942, John Hart was placed for adoption to a working-class couple. He left school at fifteen and unsuccessfully attempted to join the Surrey Constabulary. For the next six years he worked in clerical jobs while trying to improve his general education to get to university. In 1963 he studied Social Administration at the London School of Economics, and in 1965 and 1971 Applied Social Studies at the Universities of Bristol and Bradford.

Since then he has worked as a probation officer, psychiatric social worker and student counsellor. His publications include two books about sexuality: *Social Work and Sexual Conduct* (1979) and *The Theory and Practice of Homosexuality* (as co-author, 1981), as well as numerous articles. He taught for two years at Sheffield University and since 1975 has been Principal Lecturer in Social Work at Sheffield City Polytechnic, from where in 1983 he had leave of absence in order to take up an invitation to teach in Australia at the University of Sydney.

Apart from lecturing and writing, John Hart works as a counsellor in London and Sheffield, specializing in problems of sexual identity. His other interests he describes as conventional – opera (Wagner and Strauss, not Mozart), weight-lifting, listening to Radio 4 and drinking wine with friends.

Contents

Introduction

A first look at this book will give you the impression that I do not think that same-sex orientation – homosexuality or being gay – is necessarily a problem. So why should I write a book for a series which is designed to help people with personal difficulties? The answer can be illustrated by two things which happened to me during the time I was writing this book. First I was asked by a publishing firm to comment on a proposal they had received for a book to be written about discrimination against homosexuals in such areas as employment, the law, child care, etc. I responded by suggesting that such a book might not sell, as it would make very dreary reading. I then applied for a job which involved some management responsibilities as well as working with people who had a wide range of psychiatric problems in a well-known teaching hospital. Much to the surprise of the staff (who were not represented on the interviewing panel), I didn't get the post. Later I was privately assured by them that discrimination was operating to ensure I wasn't appointed. This related to my interest in writing, researching and helping people in the area of sexuality and to my open discussion of my own sexual orientation as being an important factor in such work. Now, such discrimination would not be openly admitted as prejudicing employers any more than being black or a married woman would disqualify applicants. Some local authorities now do have 'no discrimination' clauses in their job selection procedures. This is not, in my experience, to say that one is not disadvantaged, however subtly, by being openly gay, not just in employment but in many areas of social life. Having this personal experience of discrimination does not mean that I have problems about, or that I'm not happy, being gay, but it does remind me that prejudice exists and affects people even if they have (as in my case) a successful career. It is much worse if you are not yet established in work, and possibly alarming if you still feel confused about your sexuality. We shall consider in this book the social and personal costs of a *homosexual orientation* – that is, when someone's physical sexual activity, their loving feelings and their erotic fantasies are concentrated on the same sex. In doing this, we shall discover that if the problems are recognized and dealt with then the opportunities for living a satisfying and happy life are the same as for people whose sexual orientation is *heterosexual* – that is, those whose physical responses, loving feelings and erotic fantasies are concentrated on the opposite sex.

Labels such as heterosexual or 'straight', homosexual or 'gay', do not cover everyone's range of interests, and we are going to address ourselves also to the possible problems of, and the lifestyles available for, people who are not in such categories or maybe call themselves *bisexual*. They can respond in sexual behaviour, feelings and erotic fantasies towards both sexes.

Let's consider first the term 'gay'. Its widespread use now, in preference to 'homosexual', as a description of same-sex attraction, is a reminder of the importance of understanding sexual relationships at a particular time and place. In the 1980s people are still aware of negative connotations associated with 'being a homosexual', but there exists the opportunity for such people as a more visible minority to choose or rather to appropriate their own word – 'gay' – to describe themselves positively, and not just in a sexual way – after all, being heterosexual doesn't just mean what you do with your body, it also describes your total lifestyle. We should not just consider people in categories, as if 'homosexual' or 'heterosexual' could adequately describe any human being. Being called 'gay' can also be a 'political statement'. That is, it challenges traditional views of what is correct or good social behaviour, relating not just to sexual acts but also to attitudes and relationships between and among men and women. In the 1980s we live at a time when relationships between men and women are under much discussion. For some women, it is a *separate* discussion. For them, the solutions to the problems between the sexes are seen as concerning changing power relationships. It follows, therefore, that women's experiences can only be shared and made more powerful by being considered by women. In such discussions one's *sexual orientation* would be of lesser importance than one's *biological sex* as a woman or man.

I believe, however, that the approach in this book applies – with acknowledged differences – to both women and men. That is, if we do not take heterosexuality for granted, a number of common questions and situations arise which are experienced by people of both biological sexes. A good example of this is that it has often been assumed that people who have same-sex interests are not 'proper' women or men. This is because sexual orientation is confused with other aspects of sexuality which should really be considered independently. Let us set this out to clarify our understanding. We have established that:

sexual orientation is our topic; and
your *biological sex* is male or female;
your *gender identity* is whether you see yourself as male or female;
your *social sex role* is what society expects of you as a woman or man in terms of behavioural, physical and psychological attributes – such characteristics are seen as feminine or masculine.

So, for example, your sexual orientation could be heterosexual and you could see yourself as male, while in your social sex role you behave in some ways in the way expected of females – staying at home looking after house and children while your woman partner goes to work.

Alternatively, you may see yourself as homosexual, your gender identity is female and you are a full-time single parent. Or as a man you may see yourself as male and gay, like a friend of mine who goes three times a week to the gym to build up his muscles. He works on the buses as a diesel mechanic, and he comes home and keeps house for his heterosexual brother who doesn't like cooking because he thinks it is unmanly!

Being a 'proper' woman or man has got little to do with your sexual orientation and everything to do with the way we teach boys and girls to behave correctly – that is, to become part of 'heterosexual' society and to accept rigid male and female (social sex) role-playing as the only way to be. Women and men relating sexually and emotionally to each other is a challenge to all that, and it suggests that traditional social sex roles are not necessarily fulfilling everyone's potential in relationships with the opposite and the same biological sex. In order to understand the place of same-sex attraction in this we shall now consider what sexuality in general has been seen as being *for*.

Sexuality used to be thought of as primarily a human instinct which like hunger had to be satisfied; this usually applied to men – women's sexual instincts were never taken so seriously! This instinct, it was thought, should be adapted socially to ensure the survival and protection of the species by marriage and procreation. How has this changed?

From reproduction to relationships and recreation?

If we look around us at the overpopulated world of the 1980s, where sex acts do not necessarily have to be tied to reproduction, and marriage is not necessarily a once and for all thing, limiting our understanding of sex to marriage and procreation is clearly not a rich enough approach to cover most people's experience of sexuality during their lives. Many people do not just feel attraction to people of the opposite sex – heterosexuality – but also feel they can like, love and erotically respond to persons of the same sex. They may or may not act on these feelings. The reasons for this involve opportunities for meeting others, prohibitions or encouragements from the wider society and lots of individual factors. If, for example, you have always known you will marry the girl or boy next door and you want a 'family life', you may still fancy people of your own sex but your first commitment will be to heterosexual relationships. However, you may instead have grown up feeling 'different', and by the time adolescence arrives, this sense of difference has developed into the explanation: 'It's because I'm gay.' This process can happen much earlier, or later, in one's life. Some people 'always knew they were', others 'go that way' in middle age or later. I didn't come to see myself as gay until I was 30, and that wasn't the beginning or the end of my sexual interest in women or men.

Do we need sexual categories?

Am I saying, then, that everyone is capable of fancying both sexes – bisexuality – and that therefore *categories* like 'heterosexual' or 'homosexual' are outmoded? Well, I'm going to give a slightly ambiguous answer to that one! Firstly, I do think that sexuality can be seen as a way of conceptualizing or perhaps compartmentalizing certain pleasurable feelings which *could* be stimulated by thoughts of many things, including digestive biscuits, the male *or* the female human body, power, pain, success or politics!

A choice of categories?

Could anyone get hooked on any of these at random? They could in theory – the potential is there, but in practice people do not completely freely choose from the whole range of possible sexual interests. We can put it like this: I'm free to shop in Harrods or Tesco, or I can go up and down the Sainsbury's supermarket aisles and *choose* anything I like –

in theory. In practice my financial position, sex, social class, age, the law, geography and my taste buds will all ensure that what I pick up and go home with is not a 'free choice'! Undoubtedly, there is *some* element of choice in the way people come to focus sexually on the same or the opposite sex. All these elements of identifying as gay or straight add up to form a very important *filter* through which we view the world and the world, in turn, views us. Any choice is perhaps only seen to have occurred if you look back on your life and observe how a number of experiences led you to prefer relationships with the same or the opposite sex at a certain time in your life. Some idea here of fluidity – change – is implied because those factors might alter in their importance to you – for example, the socially confirming existence of family life may become of lesser importance to you as the children grow up, a marriage comes under strain or becomes routine, and a new person, who is sexually available, comes into your life. You, a married man with a flexible view of sex role behaviour (that is, you think it's OK to be tender and male), may find you are interested in the young man who has joined the squash club. As a woman you may be in a similar position (see Marcia's story, p. 79).

Our choice is here to stay?

This may be the beginning, or not, of a change in your view of your sexual orientation. Of course, a long-lasting change would be likely to be slow, because a whirlwind romance would be quite a shock in its social effects on your wife, children, friends, colleagues. Indeed, the affair may just be seen as an isolated aberration or 'the menopause'.

What I'm implying is that our sexual orientation is usually socially 'fixed', especially when there is a lot of *stigma* (that is, branding certain behaviour as 'bad' or negative or tabooed) still attached to same-sex attraction. This does, of course, work equally well the other way. Even though heterosexuality is seen as more socially rewarding, the experience of 'tainted love' is difficult to shake off except if it is seen as 'just a stage I was going through' before moving on to marriage and family life.

I am suggesting that *potentially* sexual orientation is not necessarily confined, life-long, to the same or the opposite sex, but such categories as homosexual or heterosexual do become important to people. Why is this? If same- and opposite-sex attraction, experience and interest is possible for large numbers of men and women,[1] what of those who 'decide' to have more or less exclusively homosexual identities?

Why is it only 'one in twenty'?

To answer that question, we have only to look around at the legal and social harassment of same-sex acts – the law in Britain, for example, discriminating against male homosexual acts by an age of consent being placed at 21, the name-calling which is attached to homosexual relationships by either sex – implying that those involved are not 'real' women or men – and the career disadvantages. At a time when jobs are scarce, who would wish to limit her/his opportunities further by admitting to same-sex attraction when it is frequently seen as 'putting off customers', 'offending workmates', or 'corrupting children'?

Should I 'come out' as gay?

My advice nowadays to young people wanting to get a job and yet seeing themselves as gay is to 'stay in the closet, but keep the door ajar for your friends', and this advice comes, sadly, from my own experience of discrimination. The 'spoiled identity' which is part of being seen as different tends to stick. The view that 'a leopard doesn't change his spots' may permeate a person's whole life or ensure that s/he is always seen as less eligible for promotion or trust.

Anyone who does take on the stigma of being seen as gay has to cope with social disadvantage and also of course face her/himself with the question, 'Does it make me a bad person?' 'Am I physically or mentally abnormal or perhaps even worse, deliberately perverse – upsetting my family and friends?' Not everyone will be able to answer these questions in a way which is positive, life-enhancing, giving them a good feeling about their identity and seeing themselves as a valued human being. I know people who do get disturbed about being gay and I hope this book may help. Once a person faces up to such an *identity crisis*, if you like, s/he will invest a lot in the new identity of homosexual or gay, enjoying and accepting the difference. And, to return to the question of reasons for the apparent fixity of identity – having gone through all that, few people will easily give up something so hard won. Indeed, for a variety of personal and political reasons, being seen as 'different' becomes part of one's creative self in the way one challenges traditional views of sexuality and relationships.

The legal context

As there is a law which defines the age of consent for male homosexual relations as 21 (as opposed to 16 for heterosexual acts), clearly people are going to have to be aware of this in so far as any sexual act between men which is not in private and/or in which the participants are under 21 (or in the armed forces) renders men liable for prosecution. Same-sex 'offences' are obviously under-reported to the police as they are such private areas of behaviour. In many other areas of life, people are treated as responsible adults long before they are 21.

In 1982, a private birthday party in London was raided (*Guardian* report, 20 December 1982). Thirty-seven men were arrested and kept for up to 7 hours in police cells because of a report that men under 21 were present and sexual acts were being 'committed' – this is contrary to the Sexual Offences Act of 1967 which gave homosexual men only a measure of permission to involve themselves sexually with each other in total privacy. Even though 10 weeks later these men were told none would be charged with any offence, the threat of prosecution is often around for gay men. For those who look for others in public places such as public lavatories, the results of police surveillance and subsequent prosecution can be very serious (see pages 90–91). Although not usually subject to the criminal law in respect of their homosexuality, gay women are sometimes involved with family law when questions of access to and custody of children are at stake.

Gay Legal Advice is a self-help telephone service, run by a group of gays professionally involved with the law who have built up a specialized knowledge of the way the criminal law and the law relating to employment, family matters, immigration rules and financial transactions affects the lives of homosexuals. (See Gay Signposts, page 120).

How are we going to discuss same-sex attraction?

In this book I am going to describe same-sex experiences through a number of devices, including my own experiences, some 'life histories' of people I have come to know through my counselling work, and some academic literature including something called 'sexology' – the investigation of people's sexual behaviour and theories about the causes of sexual attraction including the 'causation' of homosexuality. Such work derives from the academic disciplines of anthropology, biochemistry, psychology, sociology. A discussion of 'causes' may sound heavy to some readers, but the subject seems to be one which does often come up among gay people – and their families and friends – so I think it important that we take our own look at the ideas which are around about 'what causes it', even if only to dismiss such notions as irrelevant to the main impact of this book, which I hope will be that it is about people's lives, lives which are ordinary, but nevertheless fascinating.

Does this apply to me?

It will validate my arguments if the book describes experiences with which you can identify – whether your own orientation be gay, heterosexual, or bisexual. Perhaps only the choices you make will have been different.

How do I recognize a homosexual?

With difficulty, except if people are acting out *stereotypes*, i.e. 'camp' mincing men, or women in three-piece suits – but again, styles change, and in the 1980s, for example, gay men have been into a 'macho' look. Obviously it's in socializing places that you are most likely to meet gay people. Eye contact held for periods which are unusual in our culture is one way people recognize or express interest in each other – but that's not foolproof. A friend of mine was with some mates in a clothing shop; at the same time another man was choosing a suit. He stared at Kevin and smiled. Kevin's friends urged him to follow the guy 'as he obviously fancies you'. Out and up the street they went, the man occasionally looking round at Kevin in pursuit. He stopped to look in a shop window, Kevin closed in on him – the man turned and inquired: 'You looking for a fight, mate?'

Other options

If you see yourself as transvestite* (you enjoy putting on the clothes, the appearance of the opposite sex) or transsexual*

*There are special support groups for transvestites (see *Gay News*), and transsexuals (*Shaft*, Self Help Association for Transsexuals, 46 Liddell Way, South Ascot, Berks, SL5 9UX).

(you feel that you are in the body of the wrong sex), you may be homosexual or heterosexual or bisexual.

Am I gay?

The crucial question to ask is not about sexual acts or even just sexual interest, but 'how do you see *yourself* – homosexual, gay, heterosexual, straight, bisexual, sexual, uncommitted?'

1. *Growing up gay*

For some people, seeing themselves as homosexual, or gay, is something which seems to come to them 'naturally'. Tony, now 18, is one of the people for whom a gay identity was achieved by the time he was 14, and this experience was relatively problem-free. 'I wasn't going to fight it, that was part of me, that's what contributed to the person that I am.' This was by the time he was 14, living in a rough area and as a loner and seeing himself as 'more sensitive, and this was a contribution to being gay'. Apart from some name-calling, Tony didn't have 'any real traumas'. 'I could cope with abuse because I was comfortable with who I was.'

He was fostered as a baby along with his twin sister. 'My mum had had three miscarriages and thought (although eight years later she was proved wrong) that she could not give birth. She wanted a girl to foster but was told that she had a twin so she fostered us both and adopted us when we were three. I have got a mother and father who love me and I don't want to hurt them – or my sister – by trying to track down my "real" parents.'

These strengths and positive feelings carried Tony through the first two 'stages' of coming to a successful self-identity as being gay. (See pages 110–12.) He first admitted to himself and then to his parents his 'different' sexual orientation. Being gay was first 'a name I could attach to why I did feel different'. Two years later he told his mother. 'I was close to her and I didn't want to deceive my parents by putting on a false front. She accepted it, as I thought she would.' She told him: 'We love you and don't want to change you.' His father knows but has never spoken of it since. 'He is a typical Yorkshireman and keeps his emotions to himself.

I think deep down he would like me to get married and have children but he knows he can't change me.'

It is interesting to note here that what people have to face, and deal with successfully, is the question of what made them, their son, daughter, friend, or spouse, gay. It is not, of course, a question that is usually asked of heterosexuals.

In our society, behavioural differences are often explained as being the 'fault' of some family experience, or rather deficiency, in upbringing. Tony's experience reminds us that this 'hunt for the guilty' is neither inevitable nor necessarily helpful. 'They knew I was gay because I was the kind of person I was. Not that *they* were responsible. My mum accepted it as part of life, not a disease – it would have knocked me back if they had seen it like that.'

Tony seeing himself as different has brought some hurdles, but it is also a continuing strength in his life. 'I survived by keeping my distance. I've always wanted to leave home. It was a small village, drab and dreary, the same thing every day.' He left at 18 to live on his own in a city. For Tony, the most important way to live was to try to be himself.

Tony's encounters with 'role models', that is, people who are seen as having solid status with whom a young person could identify, strive to be like, are of interest. For people who are sexually 'different' *available* models are few and far between or are stereotypical, that is, 'nancy boys' or 'butch women truck drivers'.

For Tony, such considerations were not uppermost because 'As a kid, I didn't have stereotypes, I felt pretty certain a gay person could be anybody.' This stayed with Tony when he met gay people: 'First it was the very effeminate ones. All following each other like sheep. I had felt different at school and I felt different then. I could be friendly towards the camp little ones and I went through that. I suppose I put the bad part first – I took on superficial characteristics, all the glamour and tinsel and nothing behind it. I did feel there were people behind that façade but they didn't want to show it. I felt they didn't feel comfortable because they had to bring it out, and have it examined by other people. I wanted to shake that off and have something more. It's monotonous, repetitious, with nothing to aim for; going round in circles. I didn't want to live my life around being gay 24 hours a day – I wanted to progress.' So for Tony, going to gay pubs and clubs, having gay friends – of both sexes – is important, but he also wants a job (preferably helping other people), and he regularly works on a self-help telephone line and acts as a befriender of isolated gay people. Let's leave him to sum up, to evaluate his experience of growing up gay – to date: 'Being gay is fundamental to me as a person, it's given me strength but it doesn't rule my life.'

'When you get married and have children, this is one of the most important works for God you can do'

Jane, now 21, called herself 'lesbian' at 13. 'It was a word I knew meant attraction between women and I applied it to me. I was confused and felt this was my private moral cross which I had to bear.' Jane was at a convent, hence the language. She kept her identity to herself, and, being both a 'swot' and a rebel, managed to avoid social stigma from the other girls on the grounds of her different sexuality.

From the age of 11, Jane had been in rebellion against the social, spiritual and moral attitudes of her Catholic school, and this challenging went alongside her questioning of sexuality. The morality against which she fought is expressed in the quotation above from her 'Christian Living' lessons. Her early lack of 'conformity' was reinforced by an identification with feminism, an attitude partly fostered by her mother's views which encouraged Jane to think of having her own career, independent of men. However, her good relationship with her mother was not strong enough to prevent her mother becoming extremely upset when Jane 'came out' to her at 16. This was precipitated by Jane feeling very strongly attracted to a girl at school. 'I wanted my mother to approve; she had always been very supportive until then ... she said, "Don't be silly, it's all in your imagination. Lots of girls of your age don't feel anything towards men. It doesn't mean you're *like that*." '

Jane went on with a sexual relationship with her friend, and approached the subject again; her mother denied it, then broke down and cried. She said: 'If that's what you are, but don't tell anyone; never tell your father.'

Jane decided to tell her father. 'As he was in the police force, I thought he would be very negative. He just said: "Well I'm not at all surprised. That's all right with me. Live your life how you want to." Neither of them tried to see me as sick, although mother wondered if it was the way they had brought me up. Now we have rows about my being "out", they think it's your *private* life and you shouldn't express it. But for me there isn't a difference between the personal and the political.'

Jane didn't want to have her first relationship go on in isolation. She suggested they went to a gay pub. Her friend was unhappy about this and broke off the relationship when she went to university, saying, 'It will be easier if I try and find a boyfriend.' Jane was very depressed for a while. She then went to Europe and met up with some lesbian feminists who encouraged her to get involved in the more commercial gay and feminist scenes in England. This she did and, like Tony, she now works on a gay self-help line. 'I have relationships with women; I'm not into monogamy but I do get my feelings involved, even in the one night stands. I see myself as being a sexual person and I've never wished to be heterosexual.'

There have been difficulties in Jane's life. Her brother, three years younger, when she came out to him, called her a 'queer bastard' – but 'We never got on anyhow.' She left home but still visits her parents, with whom she has no more difficulties than many young people whose values, as expressed by their lifestyles, seem very different from another generation's. Her social circle of feminist, left-wing and gay friends keeps her identity secure as she prepares to go to university. Of the role-playing she has seen on the gay scene she says, 'I found it upsetting but I had a strong enough sense of self to distance me from it.' (See also pages 33–4.)

'Men?' There was a very depressing experience of sexual intercourse when she was 18 and drunk. 'I hated it; he didn't ask me what I wanted out of it. It was just a case of fucking me and that was it.' She had to have an abortion; 'I was very depressed before and afterwards.'

'I do have male friends, most of whom are left-wingers or are gay. I find that some gay men can be anti-sexist. My mother recently said during one of our arguments something which quite shook me: "You know if I had been born in your generation I might have been lesbian too." She sees the freedom I have, or am trying to fight for, that she would have liked, and there is some degree of envy there in her antagonism towards me.'

What's the problem?

From the stories of Jane and Tony we might conclude that 'growing up gay' is not necessarily any more of a problem than growing up is for adolescents generally. This is an important point to make to counteract any impression that being gay automatically means you are 'condemned to a life of unhappiness'. There is, however, stigma, as we have seen, to being seen as sexually different. People may have to overcome the feeling, however slight, that they are somehow sick, perverted or 'one of nature's mistakes'. Jane and Tony have shown us some of the ways in which this can be done, but obviously not everyone achieves a positive view of her/himself so easily. This may be because access to positive inputs in their lives (friends, supportive families, commercial gay scene, alternative political analysis) is not available for everyone. That can be for a variety of reasons; geographical isolation, for example, or individuals may themselves have hang-ups which mean that they can't achieve positive gay experiences with which to balance the negative ones in their lives.

Paul, now 23, is a good example of someone like this. He was born into a middle-class family, the youngest of three. The family was part of a large extended one, well known in the locality. His mother was an academic, his father an engineer.

'At primary school I was playing with girls once and a boy passed the observation that I always played with the girls and not the boys. I fobbed him off with the line that I had started early! However, even at that age, I recognized the negative things about being different. At that time the family tolerated my dressing up in my sister's clothes. I assume they thought the transvestism* would disappear, and it did when I went to state grammar school.'

At grammar school he was called names like 'queer', 'nancy', 'woman', from his early teens. On the surface this was because of his 'posh' accent. There was a lot of intimidation during his adolescence, and in defence he adopted a 'camp' style, acting superior and being 'a "New Romantic" before my time'. He recalls, for instance, sitting studying his French grammar at home surrounded by a fireguard and wearing a Louis XIV wig! This surface eccentricity was tolerated by his parents, but Paul felt inside of himself very anxious, unacceptable, viewing the world outside home and family as a frightening place to go out in on his own. In his home he felt loved and protected. Having failed to get into Oxford University, he chose a difficult four-year degree course at a provincial university in the hope of pursuing a career in the diplomatic service. He cried when he first arrived back at home after having visited his university town, and spent much of the first three years of the course returning regularly to his home and the security of his

*See page 17.

family. Socially, he remained an outsider, 'camping it up' but believing that even with his exaggerated gestures, voice and appearance no one would *really* think he was a homosexual. He saw being homosexual as a 'horrendous deviance'. Paul wanted to believe he could be heterosexual 'if I tried hard enough'.

'Every few months I would have "purges". I would decide not to look at men or think about them as I had been doing since I was 16. That was when I heard the term homosexual, before that I just felt different – just liking things girls used to like, hating football. Terribly stereotypical differences I'm afraid to say!' Paul decided to go to the Gay Society at the University, where he managed to alienate nearly everyone by giggling during a discussion about laying a pink triangle wreath on Remembrance Sunday. The pink triangle, now adopted by gays as a badge, was a Nazi insignia used during Hitler's Third Reich for those men placed in concentration camps because they were homosexual. He also referred to homosexuality as 'a condition we all suffered from', and asked, 'Does this Society help to cure it?'

Paul's ventures among homosexual women and men were occasional and, not surprisingly, unsuccessful. His own insecurity ensured he got on the wrong side of potential friends. His expressed right-wing views, membership of the Officer Training Corps and fear of being seen in public with gay friends, allied with his misery at the thought of disappointing his parents, all contributed to his remaining lonely and isolated. His camp appearance also contributed to his being assaulted by some lads one night, and he ended up in hospital where he was in fact visited by lots of people, including gays. Obviously, people could see that, beneath the façade, Paul was a person worth knowing.

Paul spent three years which he now sees as 'wasted', mostly alone, watching television in his lodgings and going home as often as possible, confining his sexuality to solitary masturbation. Occasionally, he would try to socialize. One night, for example, he went to a gay disco. On the way there he moved away from gay friends to 'chat up some girls' – 'playing straight'. At the disco he avoided meeting people, went home disgruntled, got back to his room, then decided to return to town to throw himself into socializing – only to find that the disco had almost ended and people were leaving. Paul used such experiences to confirm his 'world view' that being gay would mean unfulfilling relationships.

Three years is a long time to maintain a view of yourself as gay and 'destined' to unhappiness, and Paul invented a number of strategies to ensure that nothing really changed, including becoming obsessed with his body image. He spent long sessions with a somewhat over-indulgent university medical practitioner discussing his wish to take a course of anabolic steroids to build up his muscles. Over the period, though, Paul also began to realize that 'I was not making much progress with my "purges" and like it or not I was going to end up what we class as "a homosexual".' Somewhat reluctantly, therefore, he entered into a counselling relationship with me where he alternated between working on his need for self-acceptance and wanting to 'overcome' his homosexuality. Like many people who try to put down their sexual feelings, Paul felt his needs to be 'irrepressible – the need to have a man'. Slowly Paul did make social and sexual relationships, although he remained terrified of 'discovery' by his parents, friends, teachers. His closest friend from home and school days, the only person from school he had ever invited to his home, had also revealed himself to be a 'tortured gay', and Paul was able to take an 'older brother' kind of interest in this boy's problems. He came to see his own flight from homosexuality as a waste, and began to see his sexual orientation as a *preference*. 'Despite the horrendous disadvantages it became almost a delight to be what society saw as sexually deviant. It made it all the more appealing.'

Of course there were his 'touching wood' regrets: 'Although I came to believe a gay lifestyle to be the one compatible with the ideal future for me I did not want to alienate my family – especially my sister and any children she might have.' He also felt that he would never be able to make intimate relationships. 'It was a continuation of an old theme – either an outsider and undesirable or so genteel and courteous as to be regarded as non-sexual – only a friend' (like the relationship he had, taking afternoon tea regularly with a couple of close female friends).

What's the solution?

What these brief histories show, I hope, is that for some people, growing up gay is not a problem, while for others it may result in seemingly endless self-reproach. During such times, people may refer themselves to doctors, counsellors, friends, family, or they may keep their 'secret' burning away inside them.

There are now self-help telephone lines in most areas of Britain (see *Gay News*), so sympathetic listeners are not far away! Through these a person can be helped to take the first step, which is 'coming out' to her/himself.

And then – what's the scene?

For young people there is a Gay Society in most higher education institutions, there are teenage groups in some towns, and there is also the commercial scene, which is made up of clubs, pubs and other business ventures directed specifically at gay consumers. Most towns will have at least one pub where gay people drink. (See *Gay News*, Listings.) It is not so easy if you are female, as the clubs and pubs may appear male-dominated. A local Lesbian Line may prove helpful in suggesting alternative places for socializing. Of course, clubs and pubs require money in your pocket, and if you aren't in higher education, or if you are unemployed or an older person, then it is more difficult. A call to your local

Gay Switchboard may help, as some parts of the country have gay centres where you won't have to spend a fortune in order to meet other gay people. In addition, some Gaysocs at colleges welcome all young people, not just those who are officially studying there.

In reality the quality of self-help services varies enormously, and if you are sensitive it is easy to be put off on a first contact. The self-help groups with which I've been involved, for example, have sometimes been guilty of using social group meetings for personal socializing, forgetting that for a newcomer actually to arrive at the meeting takes a lot of effort, and that the person will need lots of reassurance that s/he *is* welcome.

Perhaps you are one of those people who can walk into a pub and get to know people – great – but be warned that gay clubs/pubs are not a guarantee of instant friendliness, and unless you can face a possible evening with no one to talk to then you had better get into gay life by a more 'formal' introduction, via contact with a Gay Switchboard.

Someone special

For some people it is more of a one-to-one first experience. They meet, fall in love with a same-sex partner, and, like their heterosexual counterparts, find this couple relationship becomes the all-important one in their lives. I suppose the differences from heterosexual pairing are few, except that the socially rewarding experiences of marriage, acknowledgement from family, friends, and the Tax Office, are not all available to the gay couple. Many different forms of gay couple relationship develop.[2] What they range from is the closed relationship – like a sexually exclusive heterosexual couple – to open relationships where no such *sexual* loyalty is expected. During the lifetime of a relationship, different arrangements may be made; that is, different agreements are reached by the partners. In the absence of the boundaries 'enjoyed' by heterosexual couples, gays have to make up their own rules in relationships as they go along. This may be the same as, more difficult, or more creative than the similar lifestyle arrangements made by heterosexuals. It depends upon the partners involved.

Help

What of people with Paul's sorts of problems? The result may be that 'coming out' is held up, perhaps for some years. People may develop a number of strategies, often exhausting for themselves and others around them, to avoid coming to terms with themselves – heterosexual boyfriends/girlfriends are one such device. Unless the heterosexual opposite sex partner 'knows the score', such relationships can have their problems.

A minority of people will 'seek a cure'. What are such persons actually seeking to achieve? Well, if it's the banishment of their sexual attraction to the same sex, they are trying to be rid of a potential held by a large number of people. If they are concerned just with sexual attraction, then bisexuality, as we shall see in Chapter 3, may be an option.

My experience, though, suggests that this will not necessarily answer people troubled about their 'homosexuality'. What one is dealing with is a pervasive feeling that they are *different* and a fear of what that means, along with distorted views of how this stops them being 'real' men or women. In other words, it's a view of themselves as total personalities, which, as in Paul's case, is the problem. It is *not* just the fact that they are erotically interested in the same sex.

I vividly remember my own experience twenty years ago when my therapist had been trying to get me to accept my homosexuality. On the suburban train, going back home from the London School of Economics, I had a vision of what I felt 'being a homosexual' meant. I would no longer be able to have a suburban semi-detached, 2.4 children and a wife. This was in the 1960s, and such things seemed very important to a working-class bloke who had managed to get to university.

Am I saying there is no cure for it? In theory, it is possible to reverse erotic preferences or perhaps more accurately revise an erotic *emphasis* from the same to the opposite sex. If someone wants this enough then presumably they will be prepared to concentrate on a heterosexual or bisexual lifestyle. They may first need counselling about anxieties they may have concerning sexual performance. (See references, page 121.)[3] Remember, though, that sexual orientation is crucial in colouring people's attitudes to life – for the gay a separate culture and/or a relationship is exciting, rewarding and *creative*. For the heterosexual the creation of a family life and the approval of society ensure that homosexuality and heterosexuality are seen as dividing people into different 'types'.

How separate are people really because of their sexual orientation?

The growing awareness of bisexuality is tending to remove some of the certainty from these issues. However, for the people involved, becoming gay or straight means living in social worlds which are at present divided. This separateness is in my view what makes change (of heterosexual or homosexual identities) so difficult, rather than it being a simple task of assuring people that, with practice and relaxation, they might relate sexually to either sex. I also know that for a number of people this latter statement is not *felt* to be true; perhaps especially so of heterosexual men and women. I respect such feelings, and, as I have already stated, I think the notion that 'everyone is bisexual' is too flippant a way of making a statement about people's potential and what they do actually achieve, given the restraints on free 'choice'.

Let's hear from Tony on the realities: 'I have a mental attraction to girls, I appreciate them. I can fall in love with men so I could imagine myself falling in love with women as well, but it's not a sexual thing. I haven't any experience of sexual relationships with girls. I suppose I'm more scared than anything. But I do feel some kind of attraction towards girls although it doesn't override my gay feelings. I suppose it might be like being scared the first couple of times I went with men but then I got right into it. Various people have told me I've got it in me to be straight as well. I don't know.'

We should also recognize that stigma must be faced if one changes from being heterosexual to homosexual. Gays who 'go straight' are sometimes also distrusted by other people – of either sexual orientation.

'My mother made me a homosexual' ... 'If I gave her the wool, would she make me one too?' – an old joke

If we talk of 'cures', we must also ask what it is that 'causes' sexual orientation. Ask yourself about the 'reasons' for homosexuality revealed in the case histories so far in this book. You may conclude that all that's revealed in the case histories so far is that people 'felt different'. If that is all, you might assume that other factors are present but have not been discussed fully – early family history, perhaps, or biological factors such as hormones or genes. I have elsewhere[4] reviewed the literature on such theories of causation. What I would indicate here is that no *one* factor explains someone's lifestyle, whether that factor is their upbringing or their genetic endowment/hormonal levels.

How *could* one such factor or even a combination of such factors explain the uniqueness of a human being? We have instead to look and see why, for each person, a homosexual, heterosexual or bisexual identity is taken on, maintained or changed over the years. To do this, we have to move beyond single factors like attraction, genetic inheritance, or reference to early psychological trauma. Such factors may be important, but only if they *mean* something to a woman or man in the way they come to see themselves. For the gay woman or man, once their 'difference' is seen as being about sexual orientation and it is accepted, then such an identity is maintained and amplified by a variety of experiences, from going to the best discos to having the right (Left!) politics.

Once the search for 'causes' is satisfied for the individual, the notion of cure abandoned, and self-acceptance begun, the potential for a creative life is possible. Let us finish with a quote from Paul: 'In quite a few of my romantic fantasies, I see myself totally gay and happy, living a gay lifestyle with another man and everybody knowing. How much of that comes true is neither here nor there – it is an image I have. At the moment, still being a student, not getting out into the world, still living in the same small circle of people, prevents that. Once I get out into the world, having got over all those traumas, I feel I can actually look forward to a gay, and happy, lifestyle.'

To summarize

Growing up gay doesn't have to be a problem. If it is, then adolescence can be a painful time as the girl or boy struggles for a good self-image. The conflicts may not be resolvable alone. A loved one may come along who can help during this time to see feelings of 'difference' as OK. Alternatively, some self-help or commercial scene experience may help people recognize that they are not alone and so begin the process of 'coming out', to themselves first, of course, and then to others. More formal counselling may be necessary if self-hatred is too entrenched, because the person may otherwise, perhaps in spite of themselves, sabotage the 'good experiences' which become available. Other gay people may be directed towards, or ask for, a way to 'cure' their sexual orientation. I have indicated the possibilities and problems inherent in such an enterprise – it is possible, but it should be seen in the context of someone's total identity and lifestyle – just think what it would mean to set out to 'cure' heterosexuality and you will see what I mean.

2. *What can two gay people do in bed?*

This is a question I have been asked by young people. For older inquirers, perhaps having already had some heterosexual experience, the question they want to ask may take the form: 'Do I have to take a certain role ("active" or "passive") in bed?'

Such first questions are understandable. The fears and anxieties are probably not radically different from those of people who are approaching heterosexual sex for the first time. Gay sex is not so much talked about, of course, and when it is it may be along the lines of 'Who is the man and who is the woman then?' This is transferring *social sex role behaviour* (see page 9) to physical encounters between people of the same sex. Such assumptions about having to play a role during sex (active – male; passive – female) are of course out of date for gays *and* straights. This does not mean that in gay sex you will not meet people who are into playing roles. What I am saying is that to enjoy same-sex acts you don't have to take on traditional male/female roles. The fact that you may, as a gay woman or man, enjoy lying back and thinking of – well, whatever turns you on – doesn't mean that you have always to play that part. Sometimes as a woman or man you may wish to snarl, growl and act aggressive. Equally OK and perhaps more realistic is just being with a partner and naturally exploring ways of pleasing each other without consciously trying to be the dominant or the submissive one. It doesn't have to be 'your turn, my turn'. Indeed, men and women going into same-sex relationships 'ought to' try to view their whole bodies as erogenous zones and get away from genitally or (more honestly) 'phallocratically' oriented sexuality. Looked at from this perspective, 'foreplay' is a redundant concept. Same-sex experiences do not have to be composed of stages in a development to 'sexual intercourse'. Each intimate, erotic act should be valued for itself and not measured against some ideal of heterosexual penetration.

When we were in bed, she said, 'What exactly do we do?'

I suppose that in theory there should be less of a problem in same-sex relationships than in opposite sexual contact. After all, you both have the same anatomy. This may not, however, counter fears of the unknown. For most people, there will have been a lot of talk with school friends or workmates about opposite-sex contact. Most first experiences of same-sex contact occur in an environment where such acts are not part of people's daily discussion.

What about fiddling around at school?

This happens a lot, perhaps more with boys than girls. I also have an impression that such 'experiments', 'playing around', 'horseplay', etc., may not be indulged in so freely by kids who are beginning to wonder about their sexual identity. That is, such casual acts like mutual masturbation may take on a more than casual meaning for certain young people, whereas the 'straight' man or woman can see early same-sex experiences as 'just fiddling about', and not as indicating a (usually stigmatized) future homosexual identity.

For people with a different view of themselves and the world, such encounters do mean more and are therefore not indulged in so lightly. People may 'want to go further' than masturbation and kiss or hug the same-sex partner. Such overtures are usually refused, and the 'future gay' returns to solitary masturbation, to the accompaniment of erotic fantasies the nature of which are kept private. Masturbation is, of course, often openly discussed by young males, and is 'justified' by the accompanying talk of opposite-sex contact. *Self*-pleasing and same-sex attraction are not usually admitted as being the reason for masturbation.

Tim, now aged 35 and gay, describes his first orgasm: 'Alone on a beach at 14 with a friend who masturbates himself.' Tim watches, says he doesn't know how to do it and his friend offers to show him. 'There was no kind of bodily contact with him, just an awareness of my own body's sensuality. I did not find him in any way sexually attractive.'

For girls such open displays may still be taboo, because of the tendency in our society to play down women's sexuality when it exists independently of men. 'Crushes', though, can certainly develop between girls, and in some same-sex schools such expressions of affection are tolerated. Same-sex acts would not be seen as so permissible.

These are really good examples of early gender differences. Affection between boys is taboo but sex acts are tolerated, while for girls the prohibitions and tolerations are the opposite. Such differences in attitudes to same-sex relationships by no means disappear in the adult lives of women and men.

Self-pleasure

> If you cannot sleep, force your thoughts into healthy channels, ... if you are unable at any time to control your thoughts, *get up, dress, and take a walk*. This is an unusual procedure, it is true, but so also is the probable alternative; and the habit of walking is at least a healthy and normal one. You need not walk far to achieve salvation, and there are few more refreshingly sane conversationists than the members of the police force on duty at night.

The above is from a chapter on 'How to Avoid "Self-

Abuse"', from a book originally published in 1925, called *The Science of Happiness*[5] (pages 270–71).

Over fifty years have not been long enough to rid us of the guilt about 'self-abuse'; again, women may be especially vulnerable to feelings that it still isn't quite right. Married people, or those with regular partners, may also feel they 'shouldn't need to'. The popular term of abuse 'wanker' shows how far we have to go to rehabilitate this universally enjoyed but often secret pleasure. I have paid some attention to this aspect of sexuality, not because it requires much skill development – although a good deal of time in people's lives is spent in practising masturbation. No, the reason is that you should go into a same-sex relationship already knowing and admitting to yourself what turns you on, so you know how to get *sexual pleasure*. Your partner should be potentially in a similar state of knowledge. All you then have to do is to exchange information.

Now there's the rub! I find that often people can't easily convey what they like (or dislike) to someone else. The reasons for this are not hard to find and are related to the taboos on self-pleasure that we have been discussing. These may result in an undervaluing or even a denial of your own body; again, this may be especially true for women. Susan: 'I was ignorant about my own body and my emotional responses, and what I was capable of.'

Just think of the things that please you, your own 'regions of delight' – breasts, nipples (men too!), anus (women too!), clitoris, vagina, penis, etc. Of course, some parts of you have yet to be discovered – not all of us can suck our own . . . toes . . . if you want an example. I shall return later to oral sex, which is probably the area we know least about before we share sex with another person.

The ways and the areas in which you stroke yourself, the rhythm, the tightness, all these are personal to you. You will have to learn to achieve equal pleasure when with a partner. Though I may seem to be going on a bit too much about self-pleasure, we must now discuss:

The dangers of masturbation

Simply put, this means recognizing that one can become so reliant on this form of sexual pleasure (especially if you have not found it easy, for whatever reason, to find a same-sex partner) that the eventual achievement of a homosexual relationship turns out to be a disappointment. This will be related to:
(1) The difficulties in communicating what turns you on;
(2) The fantasies you have built up over the, sometimes long, years.
Paul puts it like this: 'The first time may go off rather awkwardly; you have fantasized about things for so long, now you are doing them for the first time and it may be a let down.'

It is important, therefore, when going into a relationship with another person, to remember that you can always get an orgasm on your own, later if necessary. Susan says: 'At 23, I had not had an orgasm with someone else but I had spent time working hard enough on achieving this; I was just never relaxed enough.'

The likelihood is that the first time is going to be a bit fraught, but this is not necessarily because it is a homosexual experience. First-time experiences are not necessarily so hot for heterosexual young people either. Many women spend their married lives 'unsatisfied' by sex with their husbands.

'Do what comes naturally'

Relax, and don't be obsessed about orgasms or whether you will be 'active' or 'passive'. Take the general line that what you like doing to yourself the other person may also enjoy, so kiss, feel, touch the other and try risking asking her/him what s/he likes. Attend to how s/he handles *your* body; that's a clue to what s/he may be into.

If you are asked to do something you haven't tried before, try not to be negative – although there is a danger here and it is:

Innovation versus 'I've got my hang-ups'

Tony is good on this, so let's quote him: 'Don't do it if you feel it's expected of you, if you feel obliged to do it. If it feels natural, go ahead and do it.'

Ah, but if we stuck to that where would the excitement or adventure be? After all, according to 'sex experts' Masters and Johnson,[6] gay people may be more sexually responsive to their partners, in fact, 'better lovers' than heterosexuals. This must at least in part be the result of experimentation.

Michael, after 20 years' experience, suggests this attitude: 'It all depends on your reasons for not trying certain things. If it's an unwarranted fear or a misunderstanding you should try to be innovative. But if it's a real turn-off, then don't bother.'

Let's now look at some common problems

I implied that just because it is anatomically problematic, oral sex is something one comes to, usually in a state of ignorance. It isn't just that, of course; taste or an uncomfortable feeling may put people off. Susan again: 'The first time I was wondering which bit I was aiming for – I was groping about in the dark and my partner wasn't saying.'

The taste of bodily secretions is again something one may or may not get used to, likewise odours. Remember that usually it's not the reality of a 'dirty' taste or smell that may put you off, but rather what you have got inside your head: the association of ideas in which people's 'private parts' have been seen as 'dirty' and the only reason to wear clean knickers, or any knickers at all, was the statistically small risk that you might be knocked down and have to go to hospital!

Health warning

I'm not suggesting you shouldn't keep your genitals clean, and I am shocked at how few people do wash after going to the lavatory. Let us hope that the bidet is becoming less of a national giggle since we entered the Common Market. Having said this, it is also timely to add a health warning. Oral/genital and other intimate bodily contact does bring with it the risk of sexually transmitted diseases (venereal diseases). The likelihood of getting any form of venereal infection increases with the number of partners you have. Homosexual contact by both men and women may result in catching a venereal disease or infestation. This may be via the mouth, anus, or genitals. It is also possible to catch herpes on the genitals or anus, which will initially appear as painful bumps or blisters. Although sometimes you will have obvious symptoms, like sores or a discharge, this is not always so, or the infected site could be in an area you cannot see. Another complication to the 'self-diagnosis' picture is that a veneral infection *may* have non-sexual symptoms; for example, a sore throat may be assumed to be just that but can relate in fact to oral gonorrhoea. Again, diarrhoea and constipation *may* indicate the presence of a sexually transmitted disease.

Precautions against contracting sexually transmitted diseases should be part of anyone's sexual lifestyle. Proper washing of your hands and of the whole genital area with soap and water before and after sex will help; and for men, urinating afterwards is a good precaution. Taking responsibility for your body requires that you visit a 'Special' (V.D.) Clinic regularly if you are changing sexual partners.

Having said that, I am aware that going to a clinic isn't easy, and some of them, by their location (often tucked away in a prefab at the back of the main hospital), or their atmosphere (sometimes you are called up by a number and not your name), remind one of the stigma attached to all sexuality. Times are changing, however, and many genito-urinary consultants are now anxious to serve the gay community, as this is the only way to make health programmes effective.

Since 1981 an outbreak in America, later spreading to Europe, of AIDS (Acquired Immune Deficiency Syndrome), which can be lethal as it ravages the body's immune system, is causing gay men to rethink lifestyles which took for granted regular casual and anonymous sex with many different partners (see *Newsweek*, 18 April 1983).

When you visit the clinic, it is important to be truthful with the physician: s/he should know the areas of sexual contact (throat, anus, vagina, penis) so that these can be checked for possible infection. Also, you must notify your sexual partner(s) should an infection be discovered, which is why a sexual history is taken from you at the clinic. Now I know of married men who go to clinics 'passing for straight'. I hope that what I have indicated will encourage people to 'come out' so that an adequate history and examination can be made. Confidentiality is maintained in the clinics by complex filing systems so that your age, marital status and history are kept safely unavailable to people outside the Special Clinic. For information about your nearest Special Clinic, look in the telephone book under *Venereal Diseases*.*

Penetration

Gay men and lesbians do not have to penetrate any or all of the available orifices in order to enjoy good sex. Some men and women do enjoy receiving fingers, tongue, penis, others

*A comprehensive book on venereal diseases and other homosexual health problems is *The Gay Health Guide* by R. L. Rowan and P. J. Gillette, published in 1978 by Little, Brown & Co., Boston.

do not. For those people who want to be penetrated but have difficulty in allowing 'an object' into the anus or vagina, lubricating jelly (e.g. K-Y or petroleum jelly) is necessary. This is especially helpful for men, of course, who do not have the advantage of having the natural lubrication which is often available to women in the wall of the vagina.

Let me now deal with some separate problems of women and men

WOMEN – MENSTRUAL TABOO

Susan: 'Having felt withdrawn pre-menstrually, I find that I may be more aroused during my period, so for me, menstrual blood can be a turn-on.' We should realize that the fear that men had of menstruating women goes back at least as far as the Old Testament in Judaeo-Christian societies. You may well meet gay women who do not have sex during their periods, but there is no reason why you should abstain unless you want to.

MEN – 'I DON'T DO IT BECAUSE I FEEL I'M NOT BIG ENOUGH'

Size is a worry to some people. One can offer reassurance in that 'it's what you do with it that matters'. Size and shape of penis do vary a lot, but someone who is just starting gay relationships is not going to know that, of course. All that one can do is advise people not to be obsessed with such details and to remember there is usually someone who is smaller or larger than you! Those people who are the owners of micro-penises can find other ways of satisfying themselves and their partners, and anything that gets men away from being 'cock-eyed', and towards total body appreciation, is to be welcomed.

WOMEN – INORGASMIA

Ruth has a really nice relationship with Mary, but: 'I had not had an orgasm before and it was two months into our relationship before I had an orgasm. It didn't matter because we talked it out. In fact the first night it was not successful – it was so desperate and urgent – she said she thought we were sexually incompatible. But we had sex again the next morning and it was OK.'

WOMEN'S RIGHT TO SEXUAL PLEASURE

This is an ongoing battle which has to be fought both politically and in one's own mind. One of the causes has undoubtedly been ignorance of the function of the clitoris, as well as the vagina, in achievement of orgasm. Such ignorance is exacerbated by the prohibitions which surround self-exploration, and self-exploration is vital in finding the site, focus, rhythm, and abandon which contribute to orgasm. As Susan indicates above, it's 'do it yourself' then relax with the other person and hopefully it will happen – but don't count the time until it does.

MEN – IMPOTENCE (FAILURE TO GET AN ERECTION)

As there is an inordinate amount of attention and value placed upon the male organ, it is perhaps inevitable that it is not always going to 'come up to scratch'. The first thing to get right is that unless there is a physical problem, impotence is best seen as *situational*. That is, if you are able to stimulate yourself, then it's likely that it is the non-erotic turn-offs in your mind which are preventing you getting it up with other people. Now, this may be because of the demands you are making on yourself or those your partner is making, or perhaps you imagine he is making. For example, if you are mutually masturbating or kissing or biting then you may be perfectly hard, but when it comes to anal intercourse or sucking then you go limp. The cure is to stop worrying about the next act and concentrate on what you are doing. The other pleasures may come later or not at all with this particular partner. It may be that his sexual style is such that you will 'only do certain things'. It depends upon the quality of the relationship and how much you are investing in it as to how much you want to see yourself as having a 'sexual problem'.

PREMATURE EJACULATION

If coming too quickly is your problem then the above comments about worrying too much over 'performance' should also be considered.

If these problems persist, there are 'do-it-yourself' techniques which should help.[7]

This brings me to a pertinent question for both sexes: Should there be more sexual counselling for gays?

Yes – in so far as people are often kept in isolated ignorance until they enter a gay lifestyle, and old negative feelings about same-sex attraction may remain. This can result in continuing problems around having real aversions to sexuality. These problems may require counselling and some behavioural retraining.

On the other hand, the concepts that may be used in traditional 'marriage guidance' – infidelity, jealousy, sexuality focused on one person, the monotony of marriage, the need to 'give permission' for self-masturbation while enjoying intercourse, and other problems of monogamous married relationships – are plainly not always relevant to gay women and men. We will discuss gay relationships and 'casual' sex in Chapter 6, and note here that the role-centred problems encountered in monogamous marriage should not be widespread amongst gays, as each partner should be seen as more equal in the relationship, and that when penis penetration is not the index by which sexual delight is measured people can be more concerned about sharing rather than performance.

Remember, then, that the kissing doesn't have to stop! But when it does, talk about what you like today. It doesn't have to be for ever.

Age(ism)

Concerns connected with age and sexual attractiveness do occur through the gay community. For example, Marcia (quoted on page 79), a woman in middle age, did certainly feel that she would not be an attractive proposition for young gay women, and friends had to reassure her that she would be seen by many young women as an attractive person. Of course, Marcia was bringing to her new experiences her self-evaluation from traditional heterosexual relationships, where women are valued by men for their youth, low mileage and no previous owners.

Men do continue with their emphasis on youth in same-sex relationships – at least on the surface. In reality, one soon learns that relationships with age differences are quite common; indeed, as Edmund White says in *States of Desire: Travels in Gay America*[8] – gays have made adolescence last throughout life. There is no one age barrier – 25, 35, 45 – which marks the end of physical attractiveness or ability to change.

At its worst the gay, especially male gay, world mirrors all the sexual obsessions with youth and looks – people seen as commodities – of the straight society. How could it be any other way? – we are all brought up as *women* and *men*, not gays. We have to reconstruct our images of ourselves, and this does take time. It may happen at 14 or 40, in my experience. The essential task is to throw off stereotypes, but such a task is important not just for gays – as David

Fernbach[9] writes – it may be the only hope of survival on this planet.

Sexual cults

When I was at university in the 1960s/early 70s, the books I read on abnormal psychology and psychiatry all had a section entitled 'Sexual Abnormalities: Homosexuality, Sadomasochism, Transvestism, Zoophilia (bestiality)'. Therefore, in getting on to the next section I'm having to separate myself from such negative categorization in order to mention special sexual interests.

Simply because certain sexual practices which are seen as 'kinky', such as sadomasochism, were linked with homosexuality, and both were seen as 'abnormalities', one is very wary of stating the obvious fact that, like hetero- and bisexuals, and lone masturbators, homosexual men and women *are* sometimes into sexual variations. This includes sadomasochism – the deliberate integration of pain and suffering into sexual experiences. This may be mild – biting and scratching, spanking – or it may be heavier. Male gays in Britain and the US especially have recently featured such role-playing – slave/master – in leather bars. Recently, some lesbians have also taken on this interest and caused controversy about its 'political correctness'. For some women, playing such roles with another woman would be like a Jew finding an ideal home and calling it 'Dachau'.

We should accept that for some gay women and men such practices are sometimes a major sexual and social interest, while others may or may not integrate them into their bedroom scenes. Paul's attitude is instructive: 'If people say that any gay sex is wrong we might respond by thinking that if you break that initial taboo – why not do anything and everything.' Which brings us to another question.

Are gay people obsessed with sex?

A few years ago I made a video tape of a gay party which was 'custom built' for educational television. That is, it contained scenes of gay women and men kissing, dancing and what used to be called 'heavy petting'. The responses of my mostly straight audiences were varied – from 'It's boring' to 'Can we come to your next party?' This reflected the wide range of sexual behaviour which is tolerated or customary in social situations like parties and discos. This diversity in the tolerance of the open display of behaviour which was previously seen as private leads us to conclude that it is not just gay people who have sex in public places.

However, we have to take account of the restrictions on gay life. For many people, 'being gay' still means leading a secret and separate life. The tension after playing it straight all day melts away in the felt acceptance of the gay bar or other meeting place. Hence there may be only a limited time when gay sex is available, so in such circumstances when gays get together it may be that gays put more emphasis on sex. Paul says, 'When they do get together – they want it because it isn't around all the time and is seen outside as profane, so that in itself encourages people to go in for it when they are together and it's accepted.'

Sexuality, then, may be more 'in the open' in gay contacts, because of its scarcity, and because of the relief that comes from breaking down old taboos and prohibitions about same-sex attraction.

It is also important to note how difficult it is to be a gay mother, father, academic, bus conductress, politician or whatever. In other words, 'being gay' is frequently restricted to sexual acts and personal identities. Lifestyles are, in a hostile society, more difficult to establish. The other side of the coin is that society has seen gay people, especially men, as a group of people who are obsessed with sex and as purely sexual creatures. This has to some extent been taken in by the minority group itself, and acted upon. In other words, 'People see me as sexually obsessed, the opportunities are there, so I'm going to take them.' Allied to this is the restriction that has been placed upon sex in the name of reproduction. Once such a primary reason for sexual relationships is denied – as with homosexual behaviour – there seems no need to restrict its expression. We can even go further and say that, beyond monogamous pair-bonding for bringing up children, is clearly no longer central to a relationship and sexuality is no longer central to a relationship. What are the *purposes* of sexuality in such a situation? Purely recreational, I suppose, but the *meaning* placed upon sexual acts may be at odds with such a notion. In other words, sex may still be associated with security, trust, possession, power, and all of these cry out for a relationship, whether you are gay or straight or neither.

To conclude

Over the last 100 years for people of whatever sexual orientation, sexual expression has moved from the *reproductive* to the *relationship* to the *recreational*. We can all at different times see our sexual acts at differing points in this continuum. Perhaps gays are free to see, and at the same time are constrained to see, their sexuality in terms of recreational acts. So they have sex. Let's finish this section by hearing some thoughts from gay people on sex.

'It depends if you have had previous heterosexual experience. If you have, then you should know what to do.'

'You don't have to play the all-knowing man, you can ask other people to initiate you.'

'I was never incredibly attracted to the women I was with.'

'She always wanted to be butch. I wondered if the rest of the lesbian population were the same, and if so, I didn't want to know.'

'My first orgasm with a woman took me by surprise. I didn't realize what I was capable of.'

'I think promiscuity is the one common experience which brings the male gay community together.'

3. *Bisexuality*

Although there is a fair amount of ignorance about what terms like 'bisexuality' mean, if one asks people to describe someone who has sexual relations, fancies, or thinks erotically about both men and women, they might come up with a description like: 'Well, s/he is 'AC-DC', 'Swings both ways', 'Has the best of both worlds'. These all seem positive statements, and indeed in some social and political circles being able to have relationships with both sexes is seen as 'the way to be'.

Yet such environments may seem out of reach for many of the people I hear about from working on a gay telephone help line. For example, a woman who works as a housewife, has kids, and decides that she wants to have relationships with the same sex, or the man who wants to have relationships with other men but has a family life he wants to continue to enjoy and respect. How do they enter into relationships with same-sex people? As soon as they try, they then have to encounter the stigma attached to such relationships in our society, and the fact that they have a husband/wife back home may be no protection, it may even be a hardship. Gay people may see them as 'tourists', unable to face their 'true feelings' and hiding behind a marriage or opposite-sex relationship. For gay people who want to have relationships with the *opposite* sex, similar problems may exist. Clive, who at 21 sees himself as gay, developed a sexual relationship with a girlfriend which went along fine on a physical level, but he was reminded of the separation of social worlds when they went to a gay club he knew, and were at first refused admission. Clive had to describe a number of clubs he had been to before they were allowed in, having persuaded the person on the door that they were not 'just a straight couple'. This is a small incident, but it powerfully demonstrates how much social worlds may be separate, and this may prove problematic for someone who does want relationships with both sexes. It partly explains why bisexual *lifestyles* are not common, and those people who do have relationships with both sexes find it easier to keep these private or separate.

How do people manage it?

Some people can accept that they do have feelings for both sexes, but they may not call this bisexuality. They just get on with it – the gender of the person may be irrelevant. It may be justified by 'love' – perhaps especially by women – or by 'randiness' – perhaps especially by men.

People may see themselves as very sexual beings who get into close physical and/or emotional relationships without much thought for the *social meanings* that such gender differences usually bring. Kevin, at 27, is one such person. At his teacher training college he had a reputation with the girls which in some ways was a negative one. He did not always invest as much emotion in his encounters and affairs as they did. He used to 'spread it about a lot', and when this literally involved venereal disease (see pages 39–40) his reputation hit an all-time low. He had a good male friend at college who was gay, and sometimes when they went out for a drink they would finish up having sex with each other. Kevin was very attractive, so the bloke didn't mind, and no problems ensued except when Kevin suggested they had a threesome with his long-standing girlfriend Jill. The gay bloke, although he didn't dislike women, felt that if news got around the gay scene this would be bad for his image!

This is an example of how the 'stigma of heterosexuality' is preventing someone who is gay entering into non-categorized or ambivalent sexual scenes. There were no problems for Kevin and Jill. They probably still saw themselves as heterosexual; they were just having sex with another person – who happened to be male.

Some people can go on for varying periods of time having sex with both sexes, and not see themselves in any particular sexual category. This reminds us of the importance of not focusing on sexual *acts* but rather on the *meanings* they have for the people involved.

Michael and Barbara are two people who are in a heterosexual relationship with each other. Both in their early 20s, they have had relationships with the same and the opposite sex but each sees these differently. Barbara says, 'I would be kidding myself if I said I saw myself as bisexual. Even though I have had same-sex relationships, it may sound silly, but I see myself as heterosexual.' Barbara has had a number of relationships with men, including being married to one. She discovered Michael was having a secret life. He was having casual sex with men. They had talked about his previous relationships with men and women and Michael had played down his contacts with men. Barbara: 'I thought it wouldn't happen again. I was devastated when I found out – that someone could be leading two lives when I was supposed to be having an intimate relationship with him.'

This trauma made them both re-evaluate their own relationships, and 'It brought us closer together, and now if I think he is spending too much time away we discuss it and we ensure that our relationship doesn't suffer.'

The danger was that Barbara would go on being hurt by having to accommodate her male partner's lifestyle, with its attendant dangers of bringing legal and medical problems 'back home'. Fortunately this didn't happen – Michael was forced to be more open and careful about his homosexual relationships, and Barbara and he were able to share tasks around the house and commit themselves to protecting their own relationship. Also, as the couple are intentionally child-free and Barbara is pursuing her own profession, she has since been able to widen her own social life. 'People think it's "poor old Barbara" at home while Michael pursues his lifestyle; but it's not like that. I now feel freer to pursue deeper relationships with other people. Before this crisis I probably would have tried to be monogamous, but now if I have other relationships outside of my primary one with Michael then there would not be any trauma. I would tell him, it would be OK. It isn't going to split us up.'

Barbara, then, is living a heterosexual lifestyle with a heterosexual relationship which is 'open' to other relationships, and this may be with men or women – she has experienced both. Her identity is heterosexual, but, and this point is very important for our general understanding of sexuality, Barbara does not see her identity as fixed for a lifetime. She says: 'I find it hard to have relationships with men. Michael is different, he isn't into masculine or macho roles, and he is not afraid of his feminine side. I haven't given up my feminine side, I have just gained "masculine" things like automatically getting down to mending the car. If I gave up Michael I would probably go gay.'

To complete our profile of Barbara we have to see her as heterosexually identified, not sexually exclusive (monogamous), having had experiences with both men and women and being able to consider that she might, in the future, in certain circumstances come to see herself as gay. Further, she is having a relationship with a man who has relationships with both men and women, and he sees himself as 'bisexual – it's crucial to my being'. Again, this has not always been so for him. 'I have had sex with both for many years but with men I always saw it as wrong. I saw such relationships as unmanly, so I chose very carefully to limit them to *casual* encounters. I wouldn't have *relationships* with them.' Barbara adds here: 'At first you were very isolated, then you met more and more gay men and realized it was all right to be that, and that's when you realized you were OK.'

From leading a heterosexual lifestyle while having secret casual sex with men, Michael has moved to seeing himself as bisexual, although he still leads a heterosexual lifestyle living with Barbara. And the future? Like her, he would see himself having relationships with men and women, 'according to the kind of people they were'. He insists that even if his primary relationship was homosexual, not heterosexual, although he might then live a gay lifestyle, he would still see himself as bisexual.

Sometimes it has been suggested that bisexuals are really avoiding the stigma associated with homosexuality, but Michael would deny this. Certainly, because of the 'heterosexual assumption', his relationship with Barbara can be seen by their families and some friends as giving him heterosexual status. Here, identity (bisexual) is different from lifestyle (heterosexual). The problem is not what is in his own head about his identity or any fears concerning his 'real self'. He would see the lack of *integrated* social facilities to be what's wrong.

Let us sum up the social situation for this couple. The initial problem in their relationship was not, they consider, who they slept with, but getting to the point 'where you *could* sleep with other people'. After the 'devastation' of Michael's 'double life' being revealed, they were able to be more secure within their own relationship. The problems occur mostly in other people's attitudes. As Barbara says: 'Friends often don't understand. They think there must be something wrong with your primary relationship. At a party if you split up there is mutter, mutter, mutter . . .'

'At least with men you know where you stand – it's going to be awful and it's going to end unsatisfactorily. It's always a struggle.'

So far we have talked about the social problems of bisexuality and the fact that experiences with both sexes do not automatically result in someone seeing themselves as bisexual; they may see themselves as heterosexual or homosexual, or not place themselves at that moment of time in any category.

What are the features which enable someone to have relationships with both sexes, not merely write these off as adolescent exploration but rather see these as part of their potential or actual repertoire of sexual/emotional relationships/lifestyle experiences? We could contrast this with the experience of many people for whom their sexual orientation is vital to a sense of who they are.

Maureen is the author of the above quote. She is 37 and a social worker. She has a teenage son whose father is not in contact with them. She describes her sexual interests: 'Most of my experience has been with men and that is where my major interest lies. But having been involved in the women's movement and seeing the unsatisfactory nature of relationships with men – the power conflicts – I now recognize that you don't have to be dependent upon heterosexuality and your sexual interests are not determined at birth. What categories of people, what bodies you find exciting are to a large extent in your mind. So when, after living an independent existence with my son for some years, I became identified with women when I joined a women's movement group, sexual interest in them as well as men became possible.'

Maureen has, however, continued to have relationships with men. She has also had one physical relationship with a woman who saw herself as gay. As we note in her quote, she is wary of relationships with men: 'If a man isn't politically OK in his attitudes to life and me then I'm not interested.' She is also careful of entering into sexual relationships with the close women friends she has made, because 'I'm afraid of losing intimacy by taking on the sexual dimension with women.'

Maureen also has important things to say about the overemphasis on the physical aspects of sex. 'The body is only part of it. The important consideration is "Do I like this person?" I can go without sexual partners for a while. It's not a case of – if I'm not having a man I need to think about having a woman.'

When Maureen did have a relationship with a woman it was kept quiet and not admitted to friends and family, including her son. This, though, was not mainly because of Maureen's need to be seen as heterosexual, but rather the special circumstances of the relationship with that particular woman. She says it was only partly a function of worrying what the neighbours would say. 'If I had an intimate relationship with a woman in the future I would become gay. That means I would be seen openly socially as the partner of a woman.'

Maureen has discussed gay relationships with her son and thought this was important to contrast the attitudes he encounters at school where 'gay is a term of abuse'.

Maureen finds that erotically she is most interested in men, her intimate relationships are with women, and her past experience and potential for sexual relationships is with both. She is careful to place close friendships with women as important and in need of *preservation* from the possible difficulties of sexual involvement. Her 'lifestyle' remains that of an independent woman with a son, many friends and an active professional and political life. She sums up her view of her 'major' sexual experience and interest: 'I'm not the easiest person to have a relationship with. In terms of men – they don't have an easy ride with me. It's a small proportion of men who qualify.'

Maureen is certainly someone with feelings and experience about and with both men and women, but in what *category* would we place her? Perhaps her situation again reminds us of the limitations of categorization, and the importance of individual meanings for sexual experiences. We have, though, to try and answer the question of why it is that some people are able to overcome categorization of sexual orientation which is clearly so important to others. In Maureen's case it is probably very much influenced by her developing a political analysis of personal relationships. For many women, male power makes intimate relationships with men problematic. It seems logical for them to become a woman identified with women. The barriers to sexual intimacy may then recede. For Maureen it was 'slowly, very slowly. Eventually a (gay) woman came along. I saw sexual relations as a possibility. I was ready, she was around – I didn't go out and look.'

Is this kind of moving across the sexes a likely pattern for the future?

I think gender differences are important here. The women's movement may have made it politically possible or even 'right on' to love other women. This is an enormous step from seeing other women as rivals in the race to 'hook a man' who might then regard you as his possession with little right to sexual or personal fulfilment. So as we have already seen, we have women throughout their life cycle identifying as gay or having same-sex experiences, not seeing these as insignificant or psychologically peculiar, but rather as a personal and political statement of positive identity. So we can logically expect this environment to provide a sympathetic or encouraging one for same-sex relationships – among women.

Does a similar situation exist for men?

If the stigma against homosexuals is primarily about what is right and proper social sex role behaviour for men and women, as such beliefs are challenged men may come to recognize that traditional 'masculine' roles are not necessarily welcomed by women. However, part of the male role involves the assumption of male power, and this has apparently to be lost (not taken on as with feminism) if traditional attitudes to relationships are to change and barriers to same-sex relationships broken down.

Men do have on the surface a lot to lose. It may be in such

circumstances that they turn to having oppressive homosexual rather than gay equal relationships with other men. Of course, this is not automatically the outcome and the 'men's movement' contains straight, gay and bisexual men as well as those who would not be happy with any such category. In such groups, men try to *reconstruct* their identities, which were formed by early socialization into the expectation of power, competitiveness and aggression, and the putting down of loving friendships, equality, feelings and tenderness.

I would conclude that for men, same-sex relationships will continue for the majority to be taboo or evaluated as isolated from the rest of life. For a man, it requires a real sense of difference, an important gay experience, or a political 'conversion' to enable him to see same-sex involvements as part of his relationship potential. It is the *difference* which is notable, whereas for some women, although still a bit special, there is a growing belief that same-sex relationships *should* be part of one's potential.

Bisexuality must also mean less categorization for gay people, as well as 'straight', or is heterosexuality the last taboo?

In theory, this must be so, but the 'recruits' for bisexual or *ambisexual* lifestyles have come mainly from previously *heterosexually* identified people. This is likely to continue to be so. A large number of gay women have experienced, and have decided to discontinue, relationships with men. And gay men, having had to face the stigma of their masculinity being challenged and finding the rewards of a very male-oriented gay world, may find the opportunities for opposite-sex relationships not available.

Focusing on bisexuality emphasizes the importance of seeing sexual orientation as part of a sexual identity which is itself composed of a number of dimensions. If we were into 'measuring' people – Barbara and Michael, for example – we could see them on a number of 'scales' of heterosexual and homosexual feelings, interests, relationships and behaviour, and we might also assess them according to their social sex roles – that is their degree of masculinity or femininity as these assessments are so bound up with views of sexual orientation in our culture. If we believe that 'bisexuality doesn't exist', then we must recognize that we may be saying that a bisexual lifestyle doesn't exist, or is very difficult outside of certain social groups. Michael, Barbara and Maureen have many left-wing and feminist friends, which gives them an environment where traditional lifestyles, including monogamy (remaining sexually faithful to one partner) are not expected. This helps their development towards a bisexual lifestyle, even if they have to face traditional assumptions about men and women together equalling heterosexuality.

As Barbara remembers: 'Most of our support has come from gay people.' Such experiences are not guaranteed, of course – gay people may share the prejudices of straights about those who swing back and forth without apparent commitment to either identity. Knowing this may help us to understand why it is that bisexuality is either denied or distrusted. In Michael's words: 'I just do not want to be seen in a category.' We may all need categories, however, or at least we have been taught to see people in such tightly enclosed worlds. This is partly because homosexuality and heterosexuality have been evaluated differently, and the reasons for homosexuality and not heterosexuality singled out as the subject of scientific inquiry. Indeed, it is only recently that we have come to recognize that 'homosexual' is a *social role* specific to any time and place and not a universal, timeless, unavoidable description of a *type of person*. The experiences people describe in this chapter do point to the truth of this assertion.

It is often pointed out by feminists that lesbians are 'invisible' in the literature on homosexuality. We now have to go further and ask if the literature on homosexuality is in fact studying exclusively homosexuals.

MacDonald (1982)[10] makes the startling observation that a lot of the studies of 'homosexuals' use samples of men and (sometimes) women who are, in self-report, actually in some degree or other bisexual. He concludes that we may know little yet from studies of homosexuality about people who are homosexual!

What we can discover from the experiences of people in this chapter is that the existence, although often doubted, of people whose sexual interests span the sexes has been undervalued because of the tendency to see homosexuality and heterosexuality as opposites, with individuals being locked by some forceful early experience into one of these categories for ever. If we examine people's lives as we have done here we can recognize that such ways of categorizing people are inadequate. Even the major sociological studies may not take account of the range of sexual interests, but lump together people under heterosexual/homosexual categories. (See De Cecco (1982)[11], MacDonald (1982)[12].) For example, De Cecco cites Bell and Weinberg (1978)[13] who found in their study of homosexuality that 71% of their 'homosexual' respondents had engaged in heterosexual intercourse in the past. This suggests that there is more heterosexuality among 'homosexual' males and females than homosexuality among 'heterosexuals'. In this sample of 'homosexuals', 44% had feelings which were not exclusively homosexual and 26% had reported a similar attitude as expressed in behaviour.

We should also note that studies which look at sexual experience usually concentrate on 'behaviour' and 'feelings'; if one added interpersonal and other non-physical aspects of relationships, then exclusive lifelong 'heterosexuals' or 'homosexuals' would probably be very rare.

How is it then that people with a potential for interest in both sexes manage their lives? Well, probably the majority concentrate on either men or women at least during a certain period. They may also come to see their sexual orientation as fixed and unchanging, with the result that in terms of lifestyle people do enter reasonably stable roles – a minority as homosexual, a much larger group as heterosexual, and another unacknowledged group who experience interests and relationships with both sexes and may be reluctant to take on a sexual orientation identity. Although people take on heterosexual and homosexual *social roles*, we should not consider that this points to a limiting of their potential interest. Given opportunities by social change, especially in the relationship between the sexes, people will want to experiment with other sexual orientations. This is particularly true of women who are exposed to alternative political ideologies.

I have stated that the social worlds of heterosexual/homosexual are separate, but what of the 'traveller in the space between'? The people I have mentioned so far are obviously trying to live out their full potential for intimate relationships. Are there problems? Well, there can be.

The first that we should consider is the married or attached person, i.e. in a 'primary relationship'. Michael and Barbara have worked it out, but it can be more problematic. Once, while I was on telephone duty, my female colleague on a gay help line got a call from a married woman who saw herself as having 'lesbian interests'. She had told her husband but he refused to take her seriously. My colleague offered to meet this woman during the day, when she could get away from home, to talk about social facilities which might be available and how she was going to deal with her feelings. During this discussion I was amazed to hear the two of them break off from discussing how to recognize each other when the woman suddenly brought up the subject of a new royal baby, saying, 'Have you heard?' etc. The two talked excitedly about this event before returning to the woman's need for meeting lesbians. This illustrates how different worlds may collide.

For the married or committed person, either in a same- or opposite-sex relationship, other problems include:

(1) Should I tell?
(2) How do we feel about monogamy?
(3) How will this affect the life of my partner? It may give her/him the freedom to develop relationships her/himself, or it may further tie a woman to the house and children while the man is out with his boyfriends.
(4) What sort of relationships can I make with other people – how much time can I devote to them?

Sometimes people ring up who are anxious about entering into same-sex relationships – they don't want to go to local clubs and pubs because of the risks of 'being exposed as gay'. They may want to find someone for instant sex (a lot of the male participants in casual sex in public places are married men). Women may feel that the duties of family life do not give them much time to devote to relationships outside the home. It may be easier for men because traditionally they have always been expected, and have had the money, to enjoy 'a night out with the boys'. A similar facility may at present only be easily available to middle-class women in the form of a night out with a women's group.

We have learned that bisexuality is, in terms of what people self-report, a feature of many people's lives, especially if we stop focusing narrowly on sexual behaviour and feelings. Given the categories which do exist for people to pigeon-hole their sexual interest, it seems inevitable that over a lifetime, only some people will be able to move in and out of social roles as homosexual or heterosexual. This number may increase as more people become aware of the possibilities of *choice*.

Bisexuality is not for everyone, and people who are committed to homosexual or heterosexual identities may not experience or may choose to ignore their ability to respond erotically or emotionally and socially to the same or the opposite sex. Other people may alternate between same- or opposite-sex relationships, or hardly discriminate. Except in certain social groups, the latter may not know how numerous they are, as the people they meet in clubs or pubs and daily life are usually 'heterosexuals' or 'homosexuals'. Am I hinting at the social need for more groups for bisexuals to share experiences?

Undoubtedly, there are 'coming to terms' problems, as I have indicated – sex acts may appear different – fears about having to role-play. I sometimes get asked by somewhat traditional married men, 'Do you have to be the woman or the man?' Women may find it difficult to find the time or money for their own development outside the home. Homosexual men and women wanting opposite-sex relationships may have taken in the popular view that they are afraid of the genitals of the opposite sex or don't know enough about them. I reassure them that few people do, and it's easy to read about such essential knowledge.[14] Problems do exist, and are centred on separate worlds, but they are not insurmountable, and social groups do exist to help. (See *Gay News*.)

Perhaps what is needed is not more social facilities for bisexuals but, in an ideal world, less exclusively homosexual or heterosexual venues. In the shorter, more practical meantime, people who are bisexual should recognize how they are part of a heterosexual–homosexual continuum, and that there are more people with their experience than those who are exclusively interested in the same or the opposite sex. And of course, sexual acts are not the all-important aspect of anyone's identity. It is the management of lifestyle with relationships which is important.

4. *'It must be something in the water round here' – parents and children, and some discussion of the causes of homosexuality*

Gay children usually have parents who are heterosexual.

This simple statement of the obvious also highlights a possible problem; the still usual expectations of dating, marriage and grandchildren suddenly seem impossible for the father and mother learning for the first time of the sexual preference of their gay child. Of course, heterosexual children are also increasingly likely not to marry, at least for a while, married relationships may not last, and children may not be the inevitable outcome of marriage. Knowing this does not necessarily take away the initial shock of having to face the unavoidable difference represented by a homosexual son or daughter.

Is it just like any kid moving away from the nest?

We have seen already that such a 'coming out' is not always accompanied by a family crisis. We have to take account, therefore, of a number of variables in the situations of the individuals concerned. Perhaps it would be helpful to compare such likely responses with the effect of a heterosexual offspring's announcement of her/his 'growing into an adult role'. For example, a daughter's revelation that she is going to live with her boyfriend may cause very similar family tensions to those involved in facing up to her leaving home to live with a girlfriend. Both situations for a parent require:

(1) A re-evaluation of the parents' relationships.

(2) Acceptance of a child's adult sexuality.

(3) What to tell neighbours, friends, relatives.
(4) A new relationship with the young person and, where applicable, with her/his partner(s).

Similarity and difference

All of these are clearly *common* family hurdles. What are the variables? Omitted from the above list is a hurdle which is particularly significant for the parents of homosexuals. This is in my experience the inevitable question which is asked (even if it is to be dismissed, as it was by Tony's mother) – 'Where did we go wrong?'

Is it the parents' 'fault'?

This view is connected with a psychological tradition derived from *psychoanalytic theory* which emphasizes the importance of early relationships. Parents are seen as crucial to someone's ability to identify with the same-sex parent and thereby learn 'correct' social sex role behaviour, including *heterosexual* relationships. Parents may accuse themselves of having not been appropriate models for their daughter or son. This may take the form of: 'He was too close to his mother' – 'His father was too remote' – 'We always allowed her to be a tomboy'. Because of the tendency to undervalue girls' sexuality, parents of girls who are gay may not be quite so quick to make such assessments, but the felt criticism of their upbringing of a child remains. A psychoanalyst, Bieber (1962),[15] and his colleagues in North America produced the results of studying their male patients and concluded that the theory about early upbringing was true in that dominant mothers and emotionally absent fathers produced homosexual offspring. The 'oedipal confrontation' had resulted in the young male becoming afraid of women and turning to men as less frightening objects. Homosexuality was not a choice, it was a booby prize if you like, for fearful people who couldn't face heterosexual relationships, having been wounded in the oedipal conflict. Alongside this view of homosexuality is the belief that gay men and women are *afraid* or phobic about the opposite sex and are therefore psychologically disturbed.

Now the problem with this 'evidence' is that, like all the surveys of sexuality, it is not random. That is probably of less importance than the very special nature of the groups who have been studied. Bieber's group, for example, consisted of urban males heavily into psychological treatment of 'their problem'. They do not resemble the people we have met so far in this book. Furthermore, such treatments took place around twenty-five years ago and we have seen a good deal of change in attitudes to sexuality since that time. Such changes will have affected the weight of psychological and social stress borne by people who have been discriminated against. No one, for instance, would account for the public presentation and self-image of black people today in a way that referred back to the 'Uncle Tom' of stage negroes in the 1930s and 1940s. Writers still (Moberley 1983)[16] argue, from a psychoanalytic viewpoint, that gays are 'immature', but such claims should be seen in the context of their own beliefs, which can see only heterosexuality as the goal or target of human relationships.

Gay people still do seek therapy, but there are no respectable studies which show that being gay means that you are necessarily psychologically disturbed. This is a conclusion reached after reviewing the results of psychological testing of homosexuals.[17]

Certainly some gay people have problems with their sexuality and their relationships, but then so do straights. Not all gay people have disturbed family relationships, not all 'mother's boys' become gay. For some, parental experiences will be influential, but only when combined with other life experiences which serve to reinforce and develop and maintain a homosexual identity. Even if we thought that early parental modelling was powerful in determining the gender of one's sexual object choice, I find it difficult to believe that this happens in isolation from wider family–societal influences. After all, in some communities – deep sea fishing, for example – children are under the control of the mother for most of the time. Also, in our culture, 'ordinary' fathers do not spend much time with their kids. In addition, psychoanalysts argue for the oedipal or 'electra' triangle even less convincingly in explaining the development of homosexuality in women.

This is vital to our discussion, as the general neglect of lesbians cannot be fully explained without a sociological analysis of sex and power. The emphasis in examining what causes homosexuality is usually on *men*, and reflects the high value we place on masculinity and the way we devalue relationships between women separate from male power. Of course, when 'independent' women do appear as a threat, as with the publicity about lesbian mothers, then a real panic ensues among 'experts', the media, etc.

If homosexuality cannot be adequately seen as psychosocial malformation or illness, let us also consider the other common causes for it which are offered. If it is not in the (disturbed) mind, what about the body?

Is it in the chromosomes?

Except in rare cases, and even if you have a 'sex change' (whatever your sexual orientation), you will still be born with (and die) bearing XY (male) or XX (female) chromosomes. Linked to chromosomes are genes, and there is an ongoing debate among sociobiologists about the part played by genes in the development of homosexuality as an example of social behaviour as it evolves by natural selection. For an extensive discussion see Ruse (1982),[18] but do note that even if one acknowledges that genetic factors play a part in influencing who it is who goes gay, then such influences must be seen in terms of the way that resultant behaviour interacts with the individual's environmental experiences.

For example, there is a debate about genetic factors, as expressed by hormones influencing behaviour, which centres on whether girls who do have hormonal abnormalities and display tomboyish (cross-gender) behaviour are doing so because of parental mixed feelings about their gender or because of their hormonal problem. However, we should remember that such cross-sex behaviour does *not* explain homosexuals or homosexuality as we experience such people or behaviour. It merely says that hormones may contribute to boy/masculine, girl/feminine behaviours, and that certain imbalances pre- and post-natal (as measured in adult homosexuals) may cause certain *different* behaviours which are not usually associated with men or women. These may then be labelled 'pansy' and 'tomboy', and are *in our culture* often associated with homosexuality – they may also be associated with transvestism, transsexualism and 'punk' or 'new romantic'. In other words, there is not a line of direct causality which links hormonal differences with becoming and being homosexual. Also, if we make the leap to say that male and female social sex role behaviour is mirrored exactly in *sexual acts,* then we would have to assume that homosexual men play 'the woman' in acts and in fantasy and lesbians act out 'male role' fantasizing in sex, and we would have to assume that heterosexuals do not have same-sex fantasies.

None of these propositions can be described as correct. There is, however, an association reported between the *memories* of gay women and men and cross-gender social sex role behaviour. Does this mean that they were biologically determined to behave atypically in their gender role and this did result in them becoming homosexual? Well, not all homosexuals do conform as adults to effeminate or butch stereotypes. What might be happening is not the discovery of a lifetime causation but rather the *reconstruction of past events*.

Reconstruction of one's life history

This is an important factor to take account of when interpreting any findings about childhood memories. This means simply that we reinterpret our histories to fit in with current views of ourselves and our worlds. For example, if my relationship with someone breaks up I may say I really knew all along s/he was not right for me, in order to justify the time, expense and energy I put into the relationship.

I may have been called 'cissy', 'pouf', 'dyke', etc., at school and I will have as I grow up a good inkling that I'm less of a woman or man. To explain a genuine feeling of *difference* I may say, 'Well, I used to play with girls', or 'I joined a ladies' football club'. I promote such incidents which certainly may have occurred, but are now picked out and elaborated, to fit in with my current view of myself.

I am suggesting that homosexual men, especially, and women, have been in our society brought up to see homosexuality as a psychological sickness for which there must be some cause, and that they must search for this cause, to account for what is seen as their unmanly or unwomanly behaviour. Causes have been looked for in the area of family relationships and genetic/hormonal influences, and people have been taught that they are not proper men or women. People seek 'explanations' from what they have heard are the reasons – hence the 'evidence' produced.

In Spada (1979),[19] most of the American male gays stated that there was no reason why they were gay or that they were born that way. Of course, neither of these answers can be correct. There must be *some* reasons why people are gay, and being 'born that way' does not account for how you live fifteen, thirty, forty-five years later. The clue given and taken up by gay people in explaining their felt difference has been, I think, that they had problems with the opposite sex, liked dreaming/acting in cross-gender roles, were too close/too distant to mother or father, were isolated in single-sex schools or seduced or were psychologically immature or disturbed.

I hope that any discussion so far indicates to readers how only one, or a combination, of these explanations is insufficient to account for the men and women they know who have taken on gay identities. To do justice to them, we have to centre not just on sexual behaviour, which, as we have shown, many people might indulge in. What we need to take account of is the *meanings* people construct and the meanings that are available to people of their sexual feelings and behaviour. If we then look at the biographies of people who are gay and respect their experience, we will not then be tempted to interpret or reduce their life histories just to fantasized longings for parents or manifestation of hormonal abnormalities which resulted in cross-gender interests.

Gays are different

What we do have to account for is, I think, an essential experience of *difference*. In gay men and women this is linked to erotic attraction or social sex role behaviour. Such differences may come from hormonal, parental, educational, peer group, political, behavioural, fashion or moral sources. The feeling is, however, precious to a person and becomes part of her/his self identity, feeling of uniqueness, and ability to become the person s/he chooses to be.

Now the fact that the *choice* of sexual identity is sometimes denied by the person, oppressed by society, seen as morally reprehensible or as something which can't be helped, is part of the way the individual experiences the kind of society we have. Such experiences may cause stress or give a feeling of strength through opposition. This depends on the way the individual comes to see her/himself and her/his sexual orientation as part of being a woman or man in this society. Erotic interest in the same or opposite sex, the behaviours associated with being a man or woman – the things which theories of causation have sought to explain are only part of the person's sense of self. Day by day, one's lifestyle is not usually devoted to erotic acts, or gender conforming or non-conforming behaviours.

It is important to see one's difference as a uniqueness over which one has some sense of control – part of *being* the sort of person one has positively *chosen to be*. The 'fact' that the choice may be only obvious or discernible *in retrospect* does not alter its importance to the individual. In the words of the existentialist, Macquarrie (1973):[20]

> The first thing to do is simply to choose choice, to exercise the power of decision that has been so seriously eroded. Not so much the content of the decision as simply its quality as a personal act, fully and intensely appropriated by the agent, is what matters. (Page 146.)

For people who have been and become the objects of scientific research into the 'causes' of their condition, the importance of adopting this stance in relation to personal meaning is, I hope, self-evident. It is also an important stance to be offered to their parents. They may not accept such ideas, but it does move the discussion away from 'whose fault?'

After blame – what then?

Having confronted the 'Is it something we did/didn't do?' dilemma – and even perhaps having quickly dismissed the notion, what of the more common questions to be faced?

How does the boy or girl's being gay affect the following?

(1) A re-evaluation of the parents' relationships. This may be more acute because they cannot look forward to secure grandparental roles in the future.

(2) Acceptance of the child's adult sexuality. On one level, there may be little difference for parents in recognizing and dealing with their own feelings about their son or daughter sleeping with someone of the same *or* the

opposite sex. The *sexual* element may cause reverberations on to the sexual side of their marriage or relationship. This would be likely whatever the acts they imagine, or don't imagine, their children are doing.

(3) What to tell neighbours, friends, relatives. We have to face that unless it is a traditional marriage, to be advertised, then there are problems. 'She's gone to live with friends' – the safety being in the plural. As we shall see in the case example, parents may *feel* they are more exposed if it is a homosexual lifestyle their daughter/son is leading, although the decision whether to avoid, lie or accept remains the same outside of announcing a conventional (non-pregnant) wedding.

(4) A new relationship with the (young) person and sometimes their partner(s). It may be that if parents don't know any other gays they may wonder how to relate and it may threaten their own attitude to same-sex relationships (i.e. it may be easier initially to tell the opposite-sex parent, as with Jane and with Tony). But essentially it is a similar question of tolerating other people's choice of friends, their sexual expression, whatever their sex.

Now let us look at the daughter or son's contribution to the situation

We should note whether the *coming out* is self-motivated, or due to being 'found out'. Is the most sympathetic parent told first? The age of the person is important, as is their future lifestyle. Although many young people want to leave home and lead a 'freer' life, unemployment and restrictions on places in higher education may ensure this is not easily achieved. For a parent who has a good relationship with a son or daughter, their being gay may mean reassurance that they are not going to 'lose them' to a marriage relationship. Whether that staying at home is as good for the offspring, of course, is a question only answerable in individual cases.

Before meeting other gay people, 'statement of intent' may be made. Martin, now 21, made his announcement when he was 17 by leaving a copy of *Gay News* in the living-room where his mother was sure to find it. She brought it to him when he was in his room, in bed, and asked him why he hadn't told her before. There were tears, and then, at least on the surface, an acceptance. His father still does not know. His mother inquired about his sexual experience to reassure herself that he had not indulged in 'certain acts'. Such a situation highlights the importance of parental response. As the age of consent for males in Britain is 21, there is always the threat of social and legal measures to ensure that the young man does not attempt to take up a gay lifestyle. A young woman under the age of 18 faces similar potential hazards from child care legislation.[21] This is especially a problem for young people under 18, who at worst may have to fear parental threats and a reluctance by some gay groups to allow them membership because of the uncertain legal situation.

James's experience is useful to note here, because it illustrates how coming out may result in a more negative situation than keeping quiet. At 15, he lived on the coast in a remote part of England with his mother and stepfather. One summer, he met and fell in love with a man who happened to call at a near-by fishing port in his yacht. James came home with his new friend's picture, declaring to his mother and stepfather that he was gay and that this was his boyfriend. A family crisis developed, with threats of police and social service involvement unless he promised that he would forget the man and would not commit any sexual acts until he was of age. James agreed with this – he didn't have much choice. Later, he made a voluntary admission to his parents that he had gone 'straight' and had a girlfriend with whom he was in love. His private identity remained very different, and he had to content himself with reading the occasional gay novel or letter from a penfriend until he could leave home.

Mostly, of course, relationships do not undergo such dramatic reconstructions. People do just get on with life. The homosexual son or daughter either keeps quiet, leads a double life, tells the closest parent, and her/his homosexuality is accepted or tolerated, or s/he may move away. Perhaps the parents have died or are separated, or the young (or not so young) person is living many miles away from home.

What I'm saying is that sexual orientation may *not* be a long-lasting issue between generations. When it *is*, there are danger-points. The daughter may be involved in a legal custody case with a married woman with children with whom she wishes to cohabit. A son may be arrested for a public sex offence. A young person may wish to leave home to live in a town where gay socializing is more possible.

Another crisis situation increasingly brought to helping agencies involves the girl (and sometimes the boy) who has an arranged marriage on the horizon as a part of her/his ethnic group's custom. Their sexual orientation seems to them to be in conflict with generations of traditional behaviour. There is a real conflict here for individuals, and one must not be surprised, even though sad, if in such situations the person's fight for independence is given up, despite a counsellor discussing the choices which are, in theory, open to the young person.

In some families the fact of the daughter or son's gayness becomes a 'running sore' and is used as a reason for rejection. The sexual difference may also be seen as a 'deliberate way of hurting us'.

We have been through all this before – double trouble?

I am now going to discuss a situation in which it was the family's closeness which resulted in the mother, father, son, daughter and their partners all being involved in a continuing confrontation of homosexual identity. This is to illustrate how elements of such conflicts may occur and continue in some form in any family situation where same-sex orientation is a feature. It also illustrates the many factors, rather than parental inadequacy, which may result in the 'choice' of a gay identity.

Richard, now 30, saw himself as gay from adolescence, but he kept this a secret from everyone. He worked hard, both during and after leaving comprehensive school, becoming a commercial artist. He had little time for socializing beyond an occasional drink with the lads at work. At 21 he wrote: 'I seem to have spent many horrible lonely years.' He had a sister, Ruth, who was then 15. His parents were very respectable working-class people, in their 40s, his mother a conscientious housewife, his father a skilled manual worker. Their council house was immaculate.

Richard experienced very little in the way of sexual or emotional relationships before he was 21. It was almost 'by accident' that one day he went for a lunchtime drink in a city pub and met a man who within a few weeks became his lover. At first their relationship was passed off at home as 'just mates'. Then Richard and his friend decided to live together in another town and Richard felt he had to tell his parents. They had always been a close family, holidaying, going for car rides together at weekends. Sometimes Richard felt his mother was just too concerned with making sure her family wore clean knickers every day! But since she had nursed her mother suffering from terminal cancer the children and her husband had been her life. So leaving home couldn't be casual. He said: 'You know the sort of relationship it is with Allen and me, don't you?' His mother replied: 'I've had a bloody good guess!' Margaret (his mother) then tried to persuade Richard not to leave home but rather to stay and 'bring your friends here'. He didn't do that, and for a year contact between Richard and his parents was strained. They would ring him in his new home with Allen and not acknowledge that his lover was any more than someone who also answered the telephone on their son's number.

In the years that followed, Margaret continued to believe that Richard was 'going through a stage' and would return home – this Ruth reported on her occasional visits to the couple's flat. She was taking CSEs, and although brother and sister were not close, Ruth continued to visit, as relatives will do. Sometimes Richard and Allen would take Ruth to a gay disco; she didn't seem to be anxious in such surroundings, but she was always a quiet person. Richard and Allen showed no signs of splitting, and indeed challenged Margaret and George to visit them at their home and acknowledge their coupledom. This was achieved, somewhat uneasily, but perhaps no more so than with many 'in-laws'. Ruth continued to be very much at home, working close by, going home for lunch. When the occasional boyfriend called, he was scrutinized by Margaret, who still advised her on everything. The two women remained very close, were regular companions on shopping trips where Margaret advised her daughter what to wear, and they and George still went on holiday together.

Ruth was 21 when she attended a party at Richard and Allen's. It was a 'mixed' gay and straight party, and one of the less inhibited women present asked Ruth, 'Are you gay or straight?' 'I'm gay,' came the reply. The news did not sink in immediately for Richard, but when it did his first thought was, 'What are our parents going to say?' Richard and Allen felt uncomfortable because of this, and also because they had perhaps ignored Ruth's sexuality as a woman.

As neither of them believed in the 'predetermination' theory of sexual orientation, they wondered how much they had influenced Ruth's choice. Richard was a successful role model in that he had left home, had obtained a degree and had a good gay relationship and an open lifestyle. Like people do in retrospect, Richard and Allen and their friends began piecing together past events: Ruth's enthusiasm for the ladies' football team, her dissatisfaction with the local lads, the eyeing up of women in gay clubs, all seemed now to 'add up'.

In her own view, Ruth's development had its separate momentum: 'I resented Richard coming out because I realized I was going to be kept under scrutiny by our parents. I think he held me up in coming out.' At technical college, when she was 17, she had met a woman of 19 at a disco. 'I was a bit bewildered, I didn't want to acknowledge I was gay. It was just a grope behind the bicycle sheds which I thought I could bury in my mind.'

For the next 2½ years, Ruth continued going out with boys. The last one had wanted to go to bed with her so she had ended the relationship. 'After that I just went out with the girls for a drink and like them stood around looking available, but I never got involved ... The first fling I had was at another party at Richard and Allen's. It was very traumatic. I thought, "Oh, my god, is this what lesbians do – it's not done a thing for me." After that I had a relationship, but then I had an anal fissure. My mum didn't know about the relationship. I was involved with my "O" levels, and it was hard to keep anything private. During a stressful time at home, I said I was going to get a flat. My mum then in fact asked me: "You're another one like Richard, aren't you?"

'I said, "Yes, oh, yes."

' "Dad and me have thought it since three years ago when you finished with that boy."

'I had also told her at one point that I had been attracted to a girl I went to the town pubs with. I ended up crying, she ended up crying, and so did Dad. They were apologizing to me, saying: "We are sorry, we don't know how it's happened. How we managed to get two of you." It was terrible.'

Ruth's second relationship involved the family quite closely. Having been introduced to her friend by Allen, Ruth entered a stormy relationship with Viv, who was into 'femme/butch' role-playing and watched over Ruth jealously. The night before she was going on holiday with Richard, Allen and two other friends, Ruth decided to end what she saw as a restricting, clinging relationship with Viv. Unfortunately Viv wouldn't let go, and in the early hours of the morning she was forcibly ejected from Margaret and George's council house by the parents.

A year later, Ruth began a relationship with an older woman which developed into her wishing to leave home and live with her. This brought about a family crisis. Although Margaret and George had accepted and had enjoyed social occasions with Mary and Ruth, their daughter's leaving brought up many shallowly buried fears. Margaret and George rang Richard and Allen and described their conflicts: 'We just don't know what to tell the neighbours. Last time we told the closest relatives, but that's not something we're going to repeat. I think we have to protect Ruth; she is still working in the area. We just feel that it's not right going to *live* with Mary, we have bad feelings about it.'

Margaret said: 'I think people know about Richard by now, but I'm afraid they will guess about Ruth. People will ask things about her getting married, what am I going to say? You know, it isn't like having a mentally handicapped child, then one could bear the neighbours. Oh, what did we do wrong? No one seems to know what causes it. After all, you can't help being gay; perhaps its genetic, there seems to be a strong streak of it in our family. I'm disappointed, it's a shame, but there's nothing I can do about it, although I feel it's a pity you're not normal and can't get married and have children.'

Richard and Allen listened to all this and then plotted with Ruth and Mary to deal with Margaret by emphasizing her need to develop her own life now the children had left. They suggested she try to forget about 'causation' and other people's attitudes. They encouraged Margaret and George to think about their lives together. This approach can be said to have worked in so far as Margaret stopped talking about her worries.

What is interesting is that over a period of nine years, Margaret's attitude to sexual preference had not really changed. She could acknowledge, when confronted by Richard and Ruth, that heterosexuality wasn't all 'a bowl of cherries', and that she got on well with their partners and this might not have been so had her children married. But the overriding sense of shame and disappointment remained with her.

As Ruth summarizes it: 'I don't think Margaret can help it. She had always been judgemental. That's how she was brought up, in a large family which was very competitive. I don't see why in reality she is so worried about the neighbours. All she has to say is that I've left home to try and get a better job and I'm living with friends. I don't think people would press it any further.'

The ideology (belief in the rightness) of the family is very powerful in our society. Even if, or perhaps because, the imperfections of the family are well known, homosexual singles and couples are measured against this norm, and are found to be deficient. This 'deficiency' may in fact be an overt or covert challenge to the family *status quo* which may be variously faced, or confronted, or ignored, or sometimes even welcomed by parents.

I hope that this chapter, with its case histories, has illustrated the possible outcomes of family attitudes to 'gayness'. The range is as wide as I've indicated – from open acknowledgement in some cases, to years of recrimination in others – the fact of gayness may even be used to explain mental, physical or marital breakdown by parents.

Acceptance is also possible, of course! The partners of gay children may become 'honorary' sons or daughters. I know of at least one mother whose social life improved no end after being introduced to her son's gay friends.

'We still love you,' echoes dutifully round when the conversation is about 'coming out to your parents'. But of course, lots of people don't come out. 'What I do in bed is my affair' is the attitude of many. This seems reasonable enough if one views sexual orientation as only a part of life – and for many people, aware of stigma, it's a very separate part. If being gay can only mean a double life with the sexual and social kept locked away, then it would be unreasonable to demand that parents, great aunts, uncles, cousins, siblings, etc. all face this knowledge over the Christmas turkey.

I would conclude that 'voluntary' coming out to family members demands a careful evaluation of the negative and positive aspects. If the person concerned feels either themselves or their parents to be vulnerable to long- or medium-term negative responses, then it's probably best to keep quiet. If, on the other hand, a good relationship exists, then you may feel that any disruption will be temporary and you will gain the relief that positive openness creates in a more equal, less 'parent/child' relationship.

I would mention that people may feel that for 'political' reasons they should come out. That is, a gay lifestyle is seen as critical of traditional families and therefore has to be 'shouted out loud'. I think the same careful assessment of the personal/emotional costs should be made. However, such a sharing may work very well.

Marcia, married for the second time and now in her late 40s, has two daughters, now in their 20s, whom she raised as a single parent after divorcing her first husband. In the 1970s one of them revealed that she was having a gay relationship and this drew the two women closer together. It was an *enabler* for Marcia; she saw her daughter as a model for her own identification with the rights of women and the unsatisfactory nature of traditional marriage. Marcia was encouraged to rethink her own current role as the wife of a doctor. She began an affair with a younger woman, attempted to negotiate a new relationship with her husband, and with her girlfriend joined her daughters on cultural visits when she regularly visited London. Although in some ways this attempt at a new lifestyle in middle age brought Marcia more open conflicts, her relationship with her gay daughter could be seen as both enhancing their mother/daughter bond and at the same time enabling Marcia to begin to work on a new identity for herself in middle age. I should add that her husband was supportive of his wife's development.

The problems which are brought to agencies like Parents Enquiry* and to me as a counsellor are, of course, those I have already mentioned. The gay daughter or son is in conflict with her/his parents; the choice of self-revelation may or may not be available to her/him, perhaps because of age, or the law, or psychological tensions.

It is helpful to adopt the non-blame model I have outlined of sexual difference, and to emphasize that sexual orientation is a complex multi-causal part of people's relationships with each other and the world, and that happiness is not the prerogative of heterosexual or homosexual unions. To search for one factor in the family's skeleton cupboard is as limited as searching for something which caused the parents' (presumed) heterosexuality.

People's lifestyles are important, not what they do in bed, with whom, how often, etc.

Do we have to go through this alone?

It could be seen as bad luck to have two gay children. This is by no means rare. So much experience could, however, be used by all concerned to help other parents. One of the problems expressed by Margaret does relate to the *isolation* of gay parents, and groups like Parents Enquiry have been successful in getting together families to share experiences. To achieve a situation where neither parent nor child has to apologize for same-sex attraction and the 'public morality of family life' is challenged, families need to share the reality of differences which are less uncommon than they may think.

But is it just children who may be gay? What about parents?

We have discussed gay children and their parents, but there

*Parents Enquiry, 16 Honley Road, Catford, London SE6 2HZ.

are many parents in the country who themselves have homosexual or bisexual orientations. The number is unknown, but they are becoming a more visible minority. There has been a rise in the number of lesbian mothers who have applied for custody of their children at the time of divorce (Golumbok *et al.*, 1983),[22] and as the divorce rate has increased, so has the opportunity for same-sex interests become more openly admitted by previously married people. The central question is likely to be, 'Does homosexual interest make me a bad parent?' Golombok studied 37 school-age children reared in 27 lesbian households and compared them with 38 school-age children reared in 27 heterosexual single-parent households. She concluded that being brought up in a lesbian household did not of itself lead to sexual difference or psychiatric illness. She commented, 'We should cease regarding lesbian households as all the same.'

This is sound advice both to social workers and to courts who have to decide on custody cases, and to the parents themselves, whether they be lesbian or part of the smaller group, gay fathers. To help achieve this, we need to recognize that the label *homosexual* has been negatively seen as corrupting of children; people's initial reaction is that you can't be a good model for your kids. Try to forget this and recognize that the available research shows that:

(1) Offences against children are more likely to be committed by heterosexuals.
(2) It's the quality of the relationships you had before the news came out about being gay (and will continue to have afterwards) which is important in bringing up your children.
(3) Gay people are not usually afraid of relationships with the opposite sex – it's merely that they can relate intimately to their own.
(4) Children are influenced by a wide range of 'models' for behaviour, and the major message is a heterosexual one. If they see that Mum and Dad can also love people of

the same sex, that's fine – they will also know that at some time their parents (usually) will have related to the opposite sex.

(5) Access and custody are best settled out of court, as the view expressed here may be found very infrequently in our welfare and court system.

(6) Children can understand same- as well as opposite-sex attraction – they experience both. Again, it's the quality which counts, and it's important to give children positive ways of seeing gay relationships. (See Maureen's story, page 55.)

5. *Politics and sexuality*

In May/June 1981, 23% of respondents to a *Gay News* (No. 225) survey said they were in favour politically of the Conservatives. In May 1982 the Revolutionary Gay Men's Caucus[23] declared: 'We argue that capitalism has created both the conditions for the construction of homosexuality and the inevitability of our oppression.'

What can we say about gay people and politics, given such a range of opinion? The first conclusion might be that neither of these positions to the right or left necessarily appeals to the 'mass' of gays, and that political gay activists of whatever hue are in a minority. Politics is, however, about power and its distribution, and sexuality is, according to some theorists, a name we give to an activity which has come to be seen as 'not just a means of biological reproduction nor a source of harmless pleasure, but, on the contrary, has come to be seen as the central part of our being, the privileged site in which the truth of ourselves is to be found' (Weeks (1981), page 6).[24]

If sexuality is seen as so important in defining who we are, it is clearly also very influential in shaping the way that we are evaluated or given power by our society. If you think of categories like unmarried mother, promiscuous teenager, prostitute, respectable married woman/man, and homosexual, you may see the truth in the suggestion that the concept of *sexuality* carries with it the necessity of discussing its *political dimensions*. Even if the major and minor political parties appear to offer little to improve or hinder the everyday lives of gay people, most are aware that by just having the sexual label attached to them they are evaluated differently from people with other sexual preferences, sometimes in fact not as negatively. See, for example, the discussion about self-identified paedophiles (people with an erotic and affectionate interest in children) by Plummer.[25]

Are the majority of gay people aware of discrimination and oppression? I think that they are, which is why most may divide off their 'gay lives' from the rest of their day-to-day living.

Now, as we have seen, the reason for this oppression is regarded by some left-wing writers as being connected with a particular economic system – capitalism. Perhaps a larger number of people would explain their experience of legal, social and work discrimination by reference to the ignorance or fear of heterosexuals, or a belief that because of their difference, gay people are unlikely ever to be accepted by 'normal' society.

What have sympathizers and campaigners in the recent past done to change this – to achieve political power in order to reform the attitudes and treatment accorded to gay people? One of their major platforms has been putting forward the message that *gay people are the same as anyone else*; not a threat to children or family life. They would like the opportunity to become responsible members of society, instead of social or sexual outlaws. Certainly, this was a theme used in the campaign which led to the passing of the 1967 Sexual Offences Act, which provided a measure of law reform for male homosexuals. Their sexual acts became no longer illegal if they took place with consent, in private, and if both men were over the age of 21 and not in the Merchant Navy or armed forces. This Act only allowed for such 'liberal' attitudes if you lived in England and Wales. This may seem now like a minor reform but it was specifically not intended to be a platform for gay liberation: as Lord Arran, who piloted reform through the House of Lords, put it: 'I ask those who have, as it were, been in bondage and for whom the prison doors are now open to show their thanks by comporting themselves quietly and with dignity' (quoted by Weeks (1981), page 274).[26]

There was no mandate for flaunting homosexuality – the

message to homosexual men (lesbians hardly existed in the minds of the reformers) was: now you have some protection from blackmail and legal harassment, you can maintain 'normal' standards of behaviour, and keep yourselves to yourselves. Even if you cannot help what you are, there is no way in which you are authorized to present yours as an alternative lifestyle. You must make the best of having the handicap which prevents you from enjoying the happiness of normal family life.

In the 1970s, spurred by gay and other civil rights campaigns in the United States, some gay activists considered that existing measures of reform were not enough. Gay people still had not received equality before the law. Discrimination was still rife in the workplace and in the way the police operated existing laws against gays – for example, in raiding gay meeting places. The demands of gay liberation came to include not just privacy in their bedrooms but the right to present a critical view of traditional ways of living for all men and women. The rights of gays as a minority group were linked with wishes to change the position of women in and out of the family, the dominance of men and the assumption of power in so many aspects of work, political, leisure and family life. The rights of young people in general were also seen as subjugated to the authority of the family. Society was seen to be composed of groups competing unequally, and the dominance of family norms and the rigidity of the expectations of the roles to be played by men and women were seen as fostering *homophobia* – the irrational fear and/or hatred of same-sex acts and actors. The agents for this conformity were seen as the police, the church, psychiatrists and the media, and they were to be confronted not with sick, secret and insecure homosexuals but with gay and proud men and women who could testify to the rightness, not just of their sexual preference, but of an alternative way of organizing relationships among and between the sexes which was potentially available for *everyone*.

How widespread was/is a 'political analysis' of sexual orientation?

I am inclined to think that the ability to reflect on one's personal situation and see this as part of a wider public issue may be the privilege only of an élite group, whose education and employment enables them to move backwards and forwards from personal problems to political issues. In other words, I suspect that discussions of gay issues which take place in, for example, certain London bookshops over coffee are not frequently engaged in by people with only forty minutes for lunch!

So what's the common experience of people who encounter gays and politics? Well, it's possible to be surprised on the gay scene at the very low level of 'political awareness', and not just in the commercial sector. I remember my own (perhaps revealing!) embarrassment at a Polytechnic Gaysoc joint meeting with 'straight but sympathetic' left-wing friends. A young gay man announced he wasn't there for the politics. 'This is a meat market and I'm here for just that!' Examples of sexism, ageism and racism are alive and well among gays. Indeed, the way that gay women are treated by some gay men makes the average straight man in the 1980s seem less oppressive. People may be shocked by such attitudes – or they may be taken for granted as shared and common. After all, gay men and women are brought up, despite what the theorists used to claim, much like everyone else. They are likely to be exposed to views like 'My country, right or wrong', 'Women are all right in their place' – they will probably be as class- and gender-biased as the rest of society. In addition, gay people have to face the hazard of being seen as not even good at achieving the usual stereotypes of what it is to be a normal woman or man.

When I was 16, I went to work in the records office of a large psychiatric hospital. One day, I was thanking the chaplain for some helpful piece of information he had provided. 'That's very sweet of you,' I smiled. 'I'm not sweet, I'm a man,' he boomed, his deep Welsh voice rising out of his dog collar as he strode manfully to the door.

From an early age, people get the message that they are failing to live up to the expectations of normal socialization. The consequences vary for individuals – from super-conformity (some taking this as far as getting married to 'straighten themselves out') through to 'outrageous' camp personas. 'Politically' also, the results may vary from a wish to conform, to be conservative, to play down the differences, to transforming the felt personal difference into a wider view that is not just personal and individual. People may come to see their experience as part of the way society maintains stability by holding out a model of ideal family life against which people are taught to evaluate themselves. They may reject this model or keep quiet, or blame themselves if they fall short of the expectations. This applies not just to gay people but also, for example, to the large number of people who divorce and remarry.

Women particularly, because of political movements, may be able to transform their personal criticism and see it as part of society's attempts to maintain unhealthy stereotypes, including lifelong monogamous heterosexual unions, gender role regimentation – proper manly and womanly behaviour – and, particularly, the maintenance of men in a position of power in society. Given this analysis, perhaps through *consciousness-raising*, some gay people are able to come to a political view of their sexuality as being a public issue, and would no more regard their coming out publicly as inappropriately 'flaunting' their lifestyle than would the man who keeps photos of his wife and kiddies on his office desk. (See Jane's comments, page 21.)

For a minority of gay people, their work and educational position enables them to lead an *integrated gay lifestyle*, with open campaigning activities on gay rights issues, the ability to possess an openly gay persona or even to become an active spokesperson for the gay movement. In such a situation it is obviously much easier to meet and surround oneself with gay friends and lovers and enjoy social activities with other gays. Perhaps most people, though, are more middle of the road. Have the last twenty years of reform and activism brought changes to their lives . . .?

One sometimes hears older gay men and women claiming that life was better *before* the campaigning and law reforms from the 1960s onwards. This argument runs as follows. 'We were persecuted, but it gave us a minority group solidarity and an excitement in daring to live "a secret life". We enjoyed the jokes of knowing which famous people were gay. We were part of an underground resistance. The "love that dared not speak its name". Now the young people just take everything for granted.' It is understandable that as we get older we may look back with nostalgia to a more cohesive world. But even if people enjoyed the naughtiness of it all, the costs were enormous – the risks of blackmail, imprisonment and social isolation, the problems of living together openly as gay people. None of that could be compensated for by a feeling of togetherness against the world.

The rise of self-help groups providing counselling, identification, signposts and an ever-expanding gay scene now means that people can just pick up a telephone and be in touch with potentially sympathetic gay people. This is an enormous advance on the world described by West in his 1960 description of aspects of the 'gay life'.

> Entry into the camaraderie is a matter of visiting the right places in the right clothes and knowing the right conversational gambits and *doubles entendres*. A newcomer puts on just the shadow of a meaning look, remarks with just a tinge of the accepted inflection, 'Isn't it *gay* in here?' and, if he is a presentable young man, he is lonely no more.[27]

It is (thankfully) a long way from this to people wearing badges saying 'Yes, I'm homosexual too', or 'I'm one of the people my mother warned me about'. Recently a heterosexual student of mine on the second day of his work placement met a member of the staff who introduced himself by saying, 'I'm Philip and I'm gay, are you?'

If such social change has occurred, why have I gone on so much about problems?

Well, in this introductory book we are looking at a wide spectrum of people of all ages, both sexes, all classes, and of any marital status, who may be living in a range of geographical locations. Because of the inequalities in our society, it is *not* going to be equally easy to pick up that phone. When I work on a gay help line, a large number of calls are from people who, having dialled the number, can't manage to speak or later fail to turn up to arranged meetings. The facilities are there, but the fears remain – how could it be otherwise, given the gradual and uncertain pace of social change in British society.

What has occurred is that in a new generation there are *some* people for whom the situation described by West is as relevant to their experience as hearing about the lifestyle of a half-extinct tribe living up the Amazon.

What are the limits of political tolerance in Britain – it depends on what form your same-sex interest takes

In a *Guardian* report (22 July 1982), a lesbian mother who went to live with a younger woman after claiming that her husband was sexually perverted was given leave by the Court of Appeal to continue to raise her 5-year-old daughter. This may appear to be an example of social progress, but in the report the President of the High Court Family Division is quoted as saying that

> 'It was not necessary to be a psychiatrist to know that a lesbian household would be the subject of embarrassing conduct.' However, Lord Justice Watkins, who felt 'considerable unease' about

the case, also said that courts should usually only allow children to be brought up in a homosexual household when no other acceptable form of custody was available.

Is it just serious issues like the 'fitness' of a woman to bring up children which demonstrate society's limits of tolerance? From my experience it is not. I was recently involved in helping a man who was under the age of consent and who was arrested under a Public Health Act of 1936 for loitering without reasonable excuse in a public sanitary convenience. Two plainclothes policemen questioned him and warned him about hanging round a lavatory 'frequented by queers', then, apparently about to let him go, they asked his age and occupation. When he told them he was a 19-year-old child care officer they said, 'Oh, that's different.' He was summoned to appear in court. He told his employers and was sacked immediately. The solicitor he consulted advised him to: (1) Plead guilty – by letter (it is a charge unimportant enough for this); (2) See a psychiatrist. This small unproven charge changed this man's life. In a few weeks, from being a respected employee and sensitive young man he was (1) considered to be homosexual; (2) unemployed; (3) regarded as possibly psychologically disturbed; and (4) potentially a criminal! Happily, after he had consulted me and we had changed his plea to not guilty, and there had been some trade union and personal campaigning, he was found not guilty and re-employed again in social work. He was then introduced to 'less illegal ways' of meeting other gay people.

Do these two reminders of the possible legal and social hazards of being gay tell us anything about the limits of tolerance, the 'political space' which has been allocated to gay people? In the first example, we have two women bringing up a child without its father and independent of men. The opposition they faced is clearly about the unavailability of 'appropriate models' for the child, to ensure that the socialization process will produce children who will grow up knowing what is proper behaviour for them, and who they are as men and women. The fears are that a lesbian household will not do this, and, further, that a female child will be influenced to grow up seeing herself as independent of men. Only in exceptional circumstances, as a last resort, was this allowed.

In the second example, the 'iron fist in the velvet glove' was produced when the young man's age and occupation were revealed. He was then seen as a disturbed, immature person and an unfit model for the children who would be in his care. As his employers, the social services senior management, put it: 'Although he has an excellent work record during his first 9 months contract, that work and the work which he wishes to pursue in the future brings him into direct and often single contact with children. Those children are vulnerable in a number of ways and the Department may not, since it has to consider the rights and feelings of the child, the parents, and the community, take risks in some areas, even when the risk is calculated to be small.'

The limits of tolerance

We still live with the spirit of the 1967 Act, and we need to understand its premise and that this is still relevant. This can be seen in a quote from a Government Working Paper in 1979:[28]

> Most people feel that the natural and proper fulfilment of human sexuality is heterosexuality and to introduce a boy to homosexual practices may in some cases deprive him of the opportunity of a full heterosexual life. The result may be that he is committed to a life of unstable and short-lived sexual relationships. (Page 21.)

On the surface there has been change; the entertainment industry has realized what profits are to be made from the gay consumer. The expansion of gay discos also owes something to the rise in unemployment as bar consumption and attendances at 'straight' clubs, discos, etc. slump. Such public events allow gay people more space in which to pursue their social lives – *in private.*

Gay relationships also in private have now more tolerance, but this does not extend to allowing such unions the care of children. The attitude to gay people and children, whether that connection is as teacher, child care officer or parent or guardian, clearly shows how much the lifestyle is intended to be kept in check. This is especially so when 'masculinity' is threatened – demonstrated by the fears of seduction of boys by men or by the growing independence of women living free of men.

What further changes can be hoped for? Even campaigns to lower the age of male consent to 18 have still not been successful, although the 1967 Act relating to males in England and Wales has been extended to Scotland. We do not live in a time when social reform is to the forefront of government thinking. The gay movement itself is divided, without a common programme of action. The Campaign for Homosexual Equality (CHE) reflects this in that it currently has a low membership, a history of internal fighting and a division between men and women. Many women would see the feminist movement as providing a more identifiable political platform for the rights of gay women. CHE's 1982 campaigning aims presented to its annual conference seem uncertain to be realized in the next few years.

Gay charter

'Homosexual equality demands the acknowledgement that homosexuality is a valid form of sexual expression, that lesbians and gay men have the right to lifestyles free from social and legal discrimination, and that gay people make an equally valuable contribution to society. This requires:

(a) The elimination of sexism in all its forms;
(b) The positive representation in education and the media of homosexuality and the lives of gay people;

(c) The promotion of gay pride and the fostering of gay concern.'

Perhaps on its own the gay movement can never be more than a minority political voice, important in providing a platform for people whose sexual orientation still does subject them to harassment or by providing social facilities to ameliorate living in a hostile world. But on their own, gay people are unlikely to achieve much social change in the area which is crucial – that is the way that men and women relate to themselves and each other. This clearly requires a wider long-term vision than that provided by campaigns to allow a gay man to dress in leather at a local pub (an actual case in 1982) or by women having the power to exclude men from buying certain books (as occurs at one leading gay left-wing bookshop). More fundamental changes beyond the 'cosmetic' are unlikely to occur in the short-term, not because they affect the minority of people who identify as having same-sex orientation but precisely because they would affect the way women and men of every sort of sexual orientation live their lives in the last quarter of the twentieth century.

6. *Gay relationships*

We will consider:
(1) Should I have a relationship or stay single;
(2) Must it be one thing or the other;
(3) Are there other ways of living;
(4) Where are the problems of achieving relationships and what helps to make them work;
(5) What happens when they go wrong?

Some people would argue that 'a relationship' is involved even in a one-night stand. Not everyone wants to go further than that. People can search for partners (cruise) through bars and clubs – and societies – and find themselves fulfilled or unsatisfied. Those who stay home with Ms/Mr Right can also find themselves fulfilled or unsatisfied.

Being gay, there are a variety of lifestyles to choose from and you have to find one that is right for you. As Julie, someone we are to hear from later in this chapter, says, 'You have to be broad-minded to *enjoy* being gay.' There are not necessarily any blue- or pink-prints! What are the advantages of 'staying single'? Well, there is the freedom to enjoy your own life, which for young people is especially important. A single person can be involved in socializing on the gay scene without the limitations of coupledom. You shouldn't have the jealousy problems of a relationship, and you will not have the feeling that you have closed your options early. For some young women and men, getting into a same-sex relationship too early has all the problems of a 'teenage marriage', when people are forced into closed relationships while their sense of becoming individuals is still in need of a variety of social experiences. Of course, remaining single may come naturally to you if you are in higher education or living in an urban environment with lots of social opportunities. It may be less possible if you are relatively isolated geographically or otherwise not in an easy position for making friends. Then to find *someone* may be of central importance, and the disadvantages may easily be outweighed by finding someone with whom to share your life. Ronnie, in his early 20s, is a postgraduate student living in his own flat. He has a number of social and sexual relationships 'on the go'. He would like to have a close, committed relationship with a man but says, 'I should like to share a house, rather than live with him. I like to spend a lot of time on my own – so I can spend a lot of time with other people. The two have to go together. Without time on my own I wouldn't exist.' The need for space around oneself is a feeling shared by many people – so, of course, is a need to share oneself with others.

Why and how do people decide to balance these two apparently opposing needs? For some women it may be especially important to maintain their personal space, having fought so hard for this, and to continue with a sense of independence. This may be because of an earlier relationship with a man in which they were economically and perhaps also emotionally dependent, or it may be that a professional career seems to leave little room for a full-time relationship. Elizabeth is now in her late 20s and struggling to achieve her ambition of becoming a psychiatrist, having qualified in medicine. The long and irregular hours of her job and the strength of her own personality would, she recognizes, make it difficult for her to allow someone full-time into her life. Not that she doesn't have offers! As she remarks, 'Lesbians seem to arrive on your doorstep with twigs in their mouths!' Many women find her attractive; she is gregarious, sociable, fast-talking and witty, and appears, with her sports car and her flat, to be an exciting person to know. But Liz says: 'As soon as they try to get their feet under the table they are back on their bikes!' She recognizes the disadvantages – having to do all your own shopping, cleaning and cooking – but at the moment the choices available to her seem to be either a relationship with a younger or less forceful person – Liz has a very dominant personality – or a meeting of equals. She has tried both; the former she had little interest in because after a while the round of discos and parties was less important than Liz's clinical work. With an equal, Liz recognizes that they compete, and rows develop as each tries to struggle for control. She simply doesn't have that much energy left at the end of a hard day's work to maintain such a situation. 'I can't cope with stroppy relationships after a hard day at the hospital and I'm not much interested in having someone around with nothing but a pretty face.' So she remains single, not always happily so; after caring for other people, going back home to an empty flat can be depressing – and she always double-checks the doors and windows. It can be frightening on your own. But it's what Liz wants and has chosen for the last decade. She is unsure about what her 30s may bring.

There are certainly, in large cities, single 'life support systems' which provide an environment where being on your own is almost expected. You might be with a group of people who are also single, although perhaps they attach a lot of importance to each other as friends. In such groupings, they may go off to a social event with the aim of meeting each other and also seeing who is available for picking up as a sexual partner.

Michael's single lifestyle is an example of the importance of friends to single people. Now in his early 40s, he was made redundant a year ago. Although many of his friends are still working, he arranges to see a different person every day for lunch or for a drink at a gay club or pub. These regular commitments keep him from getting too desperate about his unemployment, and at present he can, just, afford to meet people socially. In a relationship he might well be isolated at home, knowing fewer people, perhaps with a lover who is in employment and having to suffer the problems of unequal financial status, or they might both be suffering the strains of living without work.

Living a single lifestyle has made twelve months of unemployment seem tolerable for Michael, and his social and sexual contacts have increased rather than diminished. This kept his morale higher than it might have been – especially when the job market sometimes tells him he is too old at 40!

But some people search continually for Mr or Ms Right and flourish in the achievement of coupledom. Take Rosie and Julie, both in their early 20s and together now for two and a half years. They are both quite clear about the central importance of a relationship. 'We like sharing and enjoying life together. We said we didn't want to be tied together, but it just happened, although we do have our own separate interests, Rosie her career, my work with various women's groups. I think straight people can be jealous of gay relationships and some people *expect* you to break up.' Rosie: 'I was talking to someone at work about our buying an expensive stereo and she said, "What if you split up?" You wouldn't say that to a married straight couple.'

I can confirm this 'double standard'. A married woman social work colleague met me after an absence of some years and asked me, 'Are you still with Richard?' I wanted to retort: 'Are you still with Arthur?' but the question wasn't expected. I assumed she would have told me if she had *not* been living with him. Julie: 'Being gay and deciding to have a relationship means that you are not bound up with rules like straights. If we hated it we could walk out.'

One of the other possible joys of a relationship is that sexual *performance* may be less of an obsession. It may become more of a balanced aspect of gay life. Julie: 'Now, gays have proved we are people, not just sex-obsessed. We don't forget sex either. We enjoy caressing and kissing, we *aren't*, though, counting our orgasms. We are making love all the time just being very physical with each other. Some gay guys seem too obsessed with scoring. You know – "I screwed three guys last week" – maybe they didn't always enjoy it.'

Assumptions (usually by men) about women and sex, are

suffered by gay women. Julie: 'The other day I went to the hospital, and this male doctor asked me, "Do you bleed when you have intercourse, do you have pain?" I said I didn't sleep with men, and when I saw his reaction I said, "You are really embarrassed now I've virtually admitted being a lesbian, but previously you weren't when asking something more personal. And to answer your question, no, I do not bleed during intercourse." He then didn't go on to ask me if I used a 12-inch vibrator every night.' Julie and Rosie both laughed at an old assumption about lesbians using 'strap-ons'. Such beliefs are connected to myths about the importance of penetration in men's views of women's sexuality – and, I would add, their own.

It may be that only in an extended relationship does one come to terms with some of one's sexual and emotional hang-ups. Certainly, connected with relationships is the idea of *emotional growth*. This is partly a takeover from certain psychological theories about the development of 'maturity'. Whether one develops or stagnates in a relationship is, I would suggest, an uncertain outcome, but undoubtedly some people do find refuge from a 'heartless world' in their own little nests, and people do also find such experiences to be ego-boosting or compensating for earlier psychological or social hurts.

Rosie again: 'I used to get so frustrated and tense at work that I used to hit her. Then I began to realize that it was because I was feeling guilty, I hadn't fully accepted myself. At home in a Yorkshire mining village I felt the only one – well, I was black and gay as well! I felt very self-conscious, deep down I think it's my colour. I used to feel everyone at home was staring at me – I liked my colour but other people didn't and that affected me.' Being with Julie slowly changed her view of herself as a person, and this included coming out as gay at work and in most other situations. 'Julie was completely out and this had made for problems in our relationship. For instance, we couldn't go out to certain places because I thought that people would see us together and think we were in love.' This emphasis on being 'out' is, I think, important in that one's *degree* of openness as a homosexual couple has important implications both for the relationship and the way you relate to the gay and straight worlds.

As Julie and Rosie point out, the degree to which you are able to come out determines to a great extent your social circle: 'We don't tend to meet closet gays. Most of our friends are openly gay.' And of course, as they illustrate, if one of you is more open than the other it can create problems.

Rob's example comes from hard reality. His job working for the government as a civil servant makes him careful about being seen as a gay person in his small home town. Felipe, his lover, has always been completely open both in Europe and in England. They share a house, have a joint bank account and are monogamous. Rob says: 'When he walks down the street with me or we go supermarket shopping and he is carrying his handbag or addressing me casually as "Darling" I just cringe.' More important, their differences in outlook resulted in them withdrawing from the gay social scene, as they failed to find a common level. Felipe wanted to be campaigning for gay rights while Rob got as far as organizing CHE coffee evenings. Of course, many other things were important to them in their relationship, but over a period of seven years of living together, Rob found himself increasingly unable to live with his fears about neighbours talking about him and he would suffer anxiety attacks when dealing with members of the public, afraid they would ask him if he was married and had a family. For Rob, the costs and risks of living what in some ways was openly as a gay couple were not compensated for by the social confirmation of gay support groups, nor, in some crucial areas, were his fears met in his primary relationship with Felipe. Here, coupledom had not overcome satisfactorily the stigma of being gay; indeed it complicated it, because Rob could not and indeed did not want to 'pass for straight' and thereby damage his relationship with Felipe. When Rob came to me for counselling, I had to help him see that he was trying to live at least half-openly as a gay man without appropriate social supports, and that over the years, his negative view of himself was resulting in him seeing himself as hopelessly neurotic and unable to cope with life, i.e. a 'sick' homosexual. I had, by advice, listening to his fears, identifying his incorrect assumptions about his own and other people's behaviour, to get him to agree with Felipe that they should 'reach out' to gay social contexts and face the risk of potential sexual encounters. I had, in other words, in a professional relationship to get Rob to change his own self-image which he had accumulated from years of knowing about the hostility which gay people face in society. He could not achieve this in his couple relationship because 'the needle had got stuck' and was playing the same tune. 'I am sick, neurotic, untrustworthy at work and unable to deal with or change my situation.'

Rob and Felipe were 'out of tune' with each other and so were unable to relate without much anxiety to the gay and straight worlds. What happens when two people try to cut off the world and live alone in their own private world? This can go on for many years with much satisfaction. I will give another example of someone who was referred to me. It is a painful story which has much to teach us.

Ian and Max met twenty-five years ago at a concert at the Royal Albert Hall. Neither of them knew any other gay people, indeed, they probably didn't call each other such names. They fell in love and remained that way, faithful to each other for the next quarter of a century. The social situation for homosexuals had changed, in some ways dramatically, during that period. Same-sex acts between men were not necessarily illegal in 1980 as they had been when they met in 1955, but this had little effect on their relationship. Ian and Max shared their lives but lived apart; both had responsible professional jobs. Max lived only a few streets away from Ian's bachelor flat; they went on holiday and spent all their spare time together. Max's only other spare-time interest was his elderly mother, whom he looked after at home until she died. No one knew their friendship was so intimate, and they knew no other gay people.

One day, Ian had a phone call from a relative of Max's letting him know that his friend had died suddenly of a heart attack. Ian couldn't tell anyone of the depth of his grief; there was no role he could take which would give him an outlet for his feelings. He just went numb; little things would hurt him, though, like a distant cousin taking over 'their' new car – he had no right to Max's estate. Ian was a quiet, hard-working, reticent man who just tried to get on with his work. His insomnia was picked up by a sensitive general practitioner, who, instead of just handing out more pills, sat Ian down and asked him why he was needing such medication. It all came out then – Ian had had suicidal thoughts and saw his feelings as so odd that he felt he must be going mad. He found himself frequently wandering back to places they had visited on holiday, and going to Wales where they planned to retire together.

Ian needed help to grieve openly – as anyone has to do when they lose a loved one – and then he had, in middle age, to build up a social life *meeting people he had never known.* It was a very difficult task to undertake, and Ian had mixed feelings about whether he wanted even to make the effort to achieve a new gay lifestyle.

After going to a couple of social support group meetings, Ian wrote to me saying he felt too uncertain about the path 'I really ought to take to continue to meet gay people socially' – at that time. It took another eighteen months before he tried again. Ian's experience is similar to that of heterosexual couples who remain 'within themselves' and have few friends to support them when one of them, 'half of them', dies. It is worse for a gay person in Ian's situation, because the 'official mourning' role is denied them. It points to the intensity and richness and 'completeness' possible in a same-sex relationship, but the costs of social isolation and not coming out, at least to yourself and close friends, as gay may have a devastating emotional (and perhaps financial) effect on the remaining partner. Private worlds are wonderful – while they last.

What happens, though, when a relationship gets into difficulties and finishes, not through death, but because one or both partners want out?

The most frequent reason is seen as sexual. Denis is white and Leroy is black. Both were in their 30s and had lived together for six years when one day Denis came home to their flat to find Leroy's belongings and his share of the furniture missing. A note announced that Leroy had fallen in love with someone else and had been having a secret affair with him for several months. Denis was shattered; he felt betrayed, unable to believe that Leroy wouldn't return to him. Fortunately, he had many friends to help him as they both were openly gay, except in their jobs which involved looking after young children. Leroy didn't return, and Denis spent many months in a dazed state, on tranquillizers. Meanwhile Leroy was apparently unaffected by the break-up, indeed he was relieved to be rid of what he saw as Denis's stifling attitude to their relationship. He felt so in love that his new relationship was carrying him through any problems of adjustment. Denis and Leroy had maintained a monogamous sexual relationship, so an extra-marital affair led to drastic steps being taken. Many couples find that it is helpful to change the rules during the length of the relationship. Over time, as the rules change, more space is created for other sexual relationships, while the other important facets of living together, including loving the other person, are continued.

The key is the *agreements* which are reached and which have to be made explicit. Are there differences between women and men here? The argument might be that the gay male couple follow a pattern common to *all* men when their lives are split between home, work, friendship, sex and love, and they have always been promiscuous. Gay women, like all women, are on the other hand home-centred, and want their sex and love and affection tied together in one person.

Another argument would be that the social life of lesbians does not emphasize casual sex, so the opportunities are less for 'shopping around'.

I think that on a very generalized level, the patterns of gender behaviour are different and are reflected in gay women placing more emphasis on monogamy than male gay couples. But again, we should be wary of categorization, especially in volatile social situations. We simply do not know what a genuine random sample of the *estimated* $2\frac{1}{2}$ million adults in the British gay community would reveal about their living arrangements at any one time.

We have discussed monogamy, living together or apart, having more open relationships, staying single. But these do not cover the whole range of possible ways of living. What about someone who has both casual sex *and* longer-term relationships? Perhaps describing such a style does more justice to the diversity of people's experiences during a lifetime. We can also ask if one precludes the other. Ronnie is someone whose experience of relationships can be instructive. Over the past five years he has had a number of sexual and sexual/emotional 'relationships' of varying intensity and length, from one-night stands 'when after an evening you have exhausted what you have in common', to those lasting several weeks, and his most important, 'the one in which for the first time in my life it was sexually and emotionally complete'. His relationship with Cliff, an American, lasted nine months and was enormously important. Previously, Ronnie had thought there was only one 'model' to try and achieve.

'I had the view that if you were going out with someone you could not have sex with anyone else! I had found the relationship I was having unsatisfying. I was still looking for Mr Right. When Cliff came along I somewhat reluctantly got involved. It started sexually. I liked him very much, and then the problems started. I wanted something defined between us. He, having left a lover at home in the States, wanted to be free. Gradually, we managed to cope with us being together emotionally and sexually and we also began having sexual relationships with other people. He taught me that you could have sex with others and not feel obliged to get other feelings involved.'

Ronnie's experience highlights the learning which can be achieved in relationships. This applied to the social, emotional and sexual aspects of knowing other people. In relation to the latter, Ronnie considers, 'I think you learn sexual techniques from several people but it's not just physical. I love meeting people and after knowing Cliff I think that socially my life with other people, gay or straight, has developed.' Cliff returned to the States. Ronnie's feelings are important to record because we all have to face that we are temporary for each other. It's a case of 'Never mind the length, feel the quality.' 'When he left I had two feelings; I felt lonely and cheated, I had given such a lot of myself to someone and I wanted it to continue. I felt the world had gone away. I drank a lot. There was another feeling, submerged for a long time, and that was of excitement. I wanted to put into practice *for myself* what I had only previously experienced in a relationship with him.' A 'deep' relationship, which is not going to last for ever, is bound to cause pain but it can be a learning, creative thing which can change your future experiences. As Ronnie says, 'Since then I have met a lot of people and had relationships, none of which were as satisfying as with Cliff, yet I know I'm idealizing. One morning at the breakfast table I wanted to stab him with the breadknife. I really hated him and I knew that I was in love. I sometimes think love is an excuse for immaturity – behaving without concern for the consequences. But I know now what I want. Relationships of every kind are becoming more important to me as I grow older. After Cliff I know now what I want and what I don't want. I wanted to get it together, all I had learned in a relationship, and put that into myself. I am looking for an emotional entanglement with someone who also wants that, *and* to be free to go on with sexual and emotional friendships with other people.'

So what works for Ronnie at this point in his history is a combination of close and casual sexual and emotional relationships. For other people, as we have seen, a lesser or greater concern with relationships works for them in their lives. For some people, like Elizabeth, close relationships would be unwelcome, out of step with the rest of their lifestyle. On the other hand, conflicts may arise for some out of wanting and 'getting into' the sort of close situations enjoyed by people I have described here.

Henry is in his late 40s, and has a really nice house of which he is justly proud. His job in teaching and his professional work take up a lot of time. He is also interested in religion, music, cooking, gardening, sailing, and learning to drive a car and ride a bicycle. In the past he has had sexual relations with women and men. Henry's lifestyle is by now fairly well established. He considers that what is missing is an intense relationship. He gets lonely at weekends and evenings sometimes, and would like to communicate intimately with a partner. However, that person would have to accommodate Henry's lifestyle, and at later stages in life we do, like Henry, establish patterns of living – including work and social commitments – which make full-time lovers difficult to accommodate.

A similar problem was faced and dealt with by Dawn. At 38 she separated from her husband, leaving the three children to live with him but still looking after them by doing the shopping and cooking, and looking after the house. She also had a job on which she worked shifts. Trying to find time for a woman lover as well as fit in these continuing commitments has meant a lot of conflicts for her. She partly resolved these by finding a younger partner who was prepared to fit in with her existing commitments and support her.

For people such as Henry and Dawn, full-time same-sex relationships may be possible only if the lover is prepared to be rather more flexible than *they* can be. On the surface it doesn't appear very equal. It is true that maintaining lots of interests, as Henry does, or having a child can get in the way.

The facts are that people do take on commitments other than just to adult relationships through life; although intimate full-time relationships may be wanted, they may be difficult to achieve.

Jim is in a different personal situation, which is common enough for us to mention here. He came to see me for counselling, complaining that he could not get close to gay men. Then 40, he had accepted himself as gay for twenty years. He had a successful and lucrative career and was a gregarious and charming person. He described how he 'froze inside' when he was in emotionally close relationships, and he had resorted to casual sex, not through choice but because of the panic he felt when people came close. He had a number of 'defences' with which he kept people at arm's length, like his ability to use words to describe how he was but also to justify himself as unable to change this. Jim was not without gay friends, but as he put it: 'If I'm invited to another gay Sunday brunch, I'll scream!' Jim related his problems to an early experience of hospitalization when he was four which had made him feel 'isolated and abandoned'. Undoubtedly this 'horror', as he put it, did have some effect on his development, but my counselling aims were to get Jim to recognize the way he used such reasons to explain why he did *not* change now, and how his 'successful' ordered life was in some ways preventing him from taking on the 'messiness' of a relationship. For Jim, a series of 'homework experiments' had to take place where he put himself in social situations (even gay Sunday brunches!) and then 'recorded' the feelings he had when someone got too close so that he could check on his inappropriate or panic signals and begin to modify these.

Any relationship taken on means losing something. Let me illustrate: some years ago when I was a student counsellor, a beautiful girl came to see me, with pre-Raphaelite looks and a lovely long dress and clean boots. She was new at the university, the first time away from home. Lonely, working most of the time, her one social activity was going horse-riding once a week. Slowly as I encouraged her she began to socialize more, and came for her counselling sessions with her hair more untidy and the boots a bit dirty. I remember having to check my own feelings of sadness that the 'unspoilt image' was being lost. She was happier, so there just wasn't time to attend to herself in the way she had before.

Relationships do cost, and each of us has to decide if it's worth it – often, perhaps fortunately, before this happens we are involved and not counting anyway!

A number of factors are present if we have to sum up a discussion of how one can relate to other gay people. Where you are in the life cycle is important, although if you are coming out for the first time at 20, 40 or 60, there may be a need to throw yourself into relationships because of the sheer relief and pent-up feelings. What happens next is, as I hope I have shown, in some ways up to individuals. You can be monogamous, live with or without your lover. Perhaps 'serial monogamy' – relating to one person at a time – whether that be days or weeks or longer – is for you, or you may decide to have a number of casual 'relationships' which perhaps should not even be called such. If you take the latter option, then my advice is to make friends with some of those lovers on the way, because you will need them as social supports.

With a lover, it's important to see the way you relate to each other as part of an open discussion. *There are no rules*, so you have to make them up as you go along. My own experience is that you should devote some time to a 'honeymoon' – that is, a period when you get used to sharing your bed or bank account without getting into a panic. Maybe later you can open up the relationship, if you agree that there is no reason to keep to a monogamous heterosexual model – unless you want to.

Perhaps unlike their heterosexual counterparts, gay women and men do have every day to ask, 'Why should I make an effort to get or keep a relationship? Why shouldn't I keep "moving on"?' The answer is that sometimes you should, but also remember that relationships are a skill which you have to develop, and as Henry found (literally as well as figuratively!), it's like learning to drive or ride a bike – as the years go by it's more difficult and the distractions of passing traffic or certain routes are more numerous.

7. *Available identities and lifestyles*

So what's different about being gay?

> *Leicester*
>
> Black lesbian, 20, amateur singer/songwriter, acoustic guitarist, seeks creative lesbian musicians including co-writer to form Afro-Spanish influenced soft rock band.
>
> Box . . . . . . *Gay News*, Number 174.

How much is the advertiser's *sexual orientation* important in this gay personal ad? For this person, being black may be very important (as with Rosie, page 98). The experience of being a woman will also be vital; for some people this might be of paramount importance in the way they experience and wish to interact with the world. Being 20 is also notable, as this woman will have been brought up in a generation that can have a political as well as a personal view of sex, race and gender (see Chapter 5). The importance of geographical location should not be under-emphasized. Outside metropolitan areas, life for gay people may offer less choice in the form of social life and people who are not just gay but also into model railways, soul, mountain climbing, or punk rock. In rural areas the needs can appear more basic, with the personal ad from a remote location crying, 'There must be someone else who is gay around here?!' Now the advertiser above is specifying *lesbian* musicians. Is this more important than the type of music? Could we assume that an

Afro-Spanish influenced *hard* rock band would be as unacceptable to the writer as non-lesbian fellow musicians? At a guess the 'common-sense' answer might be that sexual orientation is more important than musical style for this advertiser in the context of the rest of her life and aspects of her personality, and that sexual orientation does not just equal same-sex attraction and acts, but implies much more of an attitude to life – and to music!

Perhaps at this point you might like to construct a personal ad for yourself. How much weight do you end up putting on the purely sexual orientation aspects of meeting other people? How much does this vary if you see yourself as gay or not? Try constructing an advertisement with a different sexual orientation. How different is the wording? Whatever the results, it might help us to see what place sexual orientation has in our lives. Clearly there will be variations among people in the way that their sexual orientation spreads into a total lifestyle or is confined to sexual acts and interests.

So why all the fuss about being gay?

I do think that there *is* a necessity for acknowledging same-sex sexual identity. While I want to emphasize the ordinariness of the people so identified, I think there is an 'irreducible minimum' of self-awareness which has to be achieved by gay people and which is necessary for positive mental health.

I have adapted an American writer's description of *Five Stages of Same Sex Sexual Identity Development* (Coleman, 1982)[29] to clarify our discussion here. I see these stages as ones to be negotiated, however approximately, by people who are to go on to have a positive gay lifestyle.

PRE-COMING OUT

At this stage the woman or man is aware of *difference* (for whatever reason – see Chapter 4) but has not admitted it to her/himself, or conceptualized the difference as same-sex orientation. A lot of energy can be used up at this time if the person struggles to achieve a view of her/himself which fits in with her/his feelings and thoughts about relationships and lifestyles. There is a need for people to label or categorize themselves, to feel they are coming to accept themselves *as they really are*.

The flavour of such a stage may be illustrated with a personal example. Some time in the 1960s, before the arrival on the scene of discos and clubs in London, 'coffee clubs' provided meeting places for gay people. A friend and I tried to gain entrance to one of these; at the top of some stairs we met a doorman who asked if we were members. 'No.' 'Do you know anyone who is?' Again negative. We didn't get in, and we walked back down the stairs to the sound of Mama Cass singing some gutsy song to which I fantasized boys would be dancing close. I felt a real ache for something which seemed out of my reach on that and other occasions. Now I'm on the inside I know what it is, or at least I feel what the unambiguous emotions are when one feels part of a group of women and men dancing together and accepting that their difference, being gay, is taken for granted – at least in particular circumstances. Although I now think that to categorize yourself is possibly limiting and by no means inevitable, I do know the importance of achieving self-acceptance as homosexual.

COMING OUT

That's the first step – first come out to yourself, and then usually to someone else important. Their response is vital – so choose carefully because you will need their confirmation that you are still an OK person.

Next it's *exploration* time. At this point the signal has gone to green and you want to explore ways of making contact with other gay women and men. *Gay News* will give you the addresses and phone numbers of your nearest social groups, or you can use the other main signpost, Britain's 24-hour Gay Switchboard or Lesbian Line (see addresses at back). They are very well informed and helpful, and you can say thank you to them by sending a donation to keep their voluntary services running. So you get the info, you read, and then you are off . . . Is it that easy?

Not necessarily. I have already indicated that your own social situation will determine how easy or difficult you are going to find getting into a lifestyle – and how much commitment you are able to make. Let's deal with some worries.

Am I too young or too old?

No, there are teenage groups and groups for older gays in the main metropolitan centres. If you are isolated, like James (page 72) for example, it's going to be a problem, but local groups may have suggestions even if it begins with penpals.

Yes, but that's OK if I'm an attractive young person

. . . But no one wants you when you are past 30 – 40 – 50?

My experience is that this is just not true. Of course, the gay world shares the values of the straight to some extent and youth is valued, but, and this is important, gay people do feel freer to experiment with relationships which are not conventionally age-related.

We all have needs which cannot be met just by people in our own age group. People of the same age are vital so that you have a sense of finding out together, but we need also to learn from those who have 'been through it all'. We do need to go through it all ourselves, and we can then pass on that wisdom to people younger and older who have not experienced the full gay life cycle. Straight people have children and families – gay people have less access to such conventional *socializing* groupings. It is feared, of course, that gays cannot be let loose on young people because they will corrupt them. I think that would only be a concern if the example they were setting wasn't positive – by which I mean that they appeared as unhappy, guilty or neurotic, the kinds of gays in fact who used to feature in text books before we realized that they were the patients of psychiatrists and that their problem didn't originate from their sexual orientation. These were the people who sometimes gave a widespread public impression that gay people were a neurotic mess.

Someone who is positive about her/his identity will come over as such to people s/he knows – whether workmates, children at school, youth clubs, parishioners – parents are hard to convince one is happy anyway. It is certainly possible that such people will become models for identity as gay people. But whether that is related just to their sexual orientation is much less likely. The development of that facet of a person is, as we have discussed, so bound up with the total messages people get and act upon about what is right and proper behaviour for a woman or man in our society. I am not saying that knowing someone gay will not affect you. If, after hearing all the negative things about same-sex attraction from people at school, the media and other 'authorities', a young person meets someone who is gay, and is not a child molester, spy, or pervert but a positive happy person, and they think they wouldn't mind being like them – we could hardly call this corruption, could we?

Yes, but you are preventing them enjoying a family

Well, not necessarily so. Lesbian mothers have been widely featured in the press, and a large number of gays of both sexes are parents – groups now exist to support them.

But this isn't the ideal typical family life my religion tells me is right

This is a problem, but there are now gay groups identifying the major faiths – Catholic, Jewish, Quaker and Evangelical! – who could debate this with you. Their addresses are available from the signposts I've already given.

So if you do then feel free enough to explore, you may need to find a number of relationships rather than one (see Chapter 6). Just don't panic if you find yourself having a bit of a wild time, especially if this seems inappropriate for someone of your mature years! Recognize it for what it is – a release of pressure when you can try out what have previously been lonely fantasies. At best you should get your sexual feelings in perspective – they may have taken over rather like Paul's (page 25). After all, this may have been the only way you saw being gay. Working on a help line, I find it's a familiar first call from quite young people who want to meet another gay person. When one offers this they may ask, 'Will I be able to hold you or kiss you?' – this is more likely in men, but women are now also being able to express their sexual wants. Such questions deserve very careful handling to prevent the person feeling rejected while making clear the distinctions between befriending, which is what one is offering, and a sexual service. One has to remember that sex acts may be the only way some people see same-sex orientation.

A wider awareness of lifestyle comes later, or as people develop after such initial sexual exploration is achieved. At this point, a frequent worry that I hear from young men and women is about their sexual behaviour. As part of this stage they may explore a number of sexual relationships and then think they are getting a reputation as a 'tart', with the result that they decide to give it all up. To themselves or close friends they may confide that 'There isn't going to be any tongue kissing until I fall in love' or 'I'm not letting anyone go any further until we are having a longer-term relationship.' Such reactions are understandable when someone is struggling to balance her/his new-found sexual freedom with an association of 'promiscuous' sexual behaviour with 'being cheap' and therefore not respected by others – or oneself. There are a number of ways to solve this worry – give up sex, or put sex in the context of a close emotional relationship. It may also be that as time goes by, sexual acts become less connected with the way you evaluate your whole personality. Being good at your job, having real friends, being a good dancer, may be more important than how often you do what with whom!

According to Coleman: 'When gay men and lesbians conceive of themselves as capable of loving and being loved, they are ready to enter this next stage of first relationships.'

FIRST RELATIONSHIPS

I'm unsure about such definite statements as Coleman's (see Chapter 6), but for those people who do decide on a lifestyle of intimate one to ones (at a time, anyway!), we should note that the person may find s/he has so much to give and get that the relationship is a fraught one, with restrictions and jealousy near the surface *as well as* – as Ronnie (pages 103–5) puts it – 'Being in love means you are whistling in the morning.'

People and relationships can change, and especially helpful is the support of the gay community. John is an example of someone who never achieved this. At a very young age he was picked up by an older person who was himself involved in a long-term relationship. He was well off and installed John and his sister in a house, providing them with instant separation from the parental home and a lifestyle involving many comforts. Unfortunately, John was still in the process of coming out to himself and he still has not achieved this, four years on. So at work he stays the 'super macho man' with the girls, and maintains his part-time but now financially and emotionally dependent relationship with someone who has no intention of leaving the man he lives with. John is not content, but he never appears on the gay scene and uses casual sex in pick-up places to supplement his one gay intimate contact.

The warning of John's history is that a first relationship may be restricting unless one is able to use it to come to terms with one's own identity, rather than to foreclose on it by shutting off from other gay socializing and identifying.

After the turbulence of a first relationship the gay person may be left feeling that such intimacies with one person are not for them, or they may carry on in a similar pattern to John, not really in and not really out of a relationship, or not establishing a gay identity. Others may feel able to move on to the 'next stage'.

INTEGRATION

Here a good image of yourself is achieved and you see yourself as capable of relationships *as a gay person*, but not needing these in a dependent or clinging way for holding yourself together. As Ronnie (page 104) says: '. . . I know now what I want and don't want. I wanted to get it together, all I had learned in a relationship, and put that into myself.' Of course, one goes on after this, facing the life cycle, adulthood, middle and old age, but with a feeling that you know who you are (self-awareness) and you like yourself for what you are.

As we have seen in this book, the resultant lifestyles vary enormously. Having acknowledged the common need to achieve a same-sex identity, the lifestyles are diverse. Indeed, as the personal ad at the beginning of the chapter is dissected, the common denominator of sexual orientation soon gets mixed into the other parts of people's interests and lives – their age, gender, race, class, marital status, geographical location and personal and political interests.

Do you have a choice as to how much importance being

attracted to the same sex has in your life? Any such choice is going to be affected by all the factors above, not necessarily in the conventional way of only meeting people of your own class. Being gay does to some extent enable people to cross class, age, and racial boundaries. Some barriers – like black/white – can be leapt across successfully. But we are all living in a society which practises racism, sexism and ageism, and in spite of the fact that gay relationships and identities can and do give people new awareness of oppression they cannot, as we saw in the last chapters, achieve any massive permanent change in the way that people maintain unequal relationships. The restrictions will continue to be there. For instance, if you are a married woman with children, it may be no more easy to have a relationship outside the home with a woman than it would be with a man.

If you do choose a same-sex relationship, given it's the same social world you live in, will you be happier if you have previously been unhappy? As Susan puts it: 'Before I met gay people I got so lonely and unhappy I thought nothing could be so bad. I had nothing to lose.' For Susan, getting involved with other gays was what she wanted and Susan was happier for having made the step. Although people can have the experience of getting into the gay scene, heaving a sigh and saying, 'I'm home', the 'gay world' is part of the rest of society and reflects many of the problems of all human beings trying to find lifestyles which can cope with personal anxieties, structural unemployment, the threat of personal and inter-group violence, and a multiplicity of other factors encompassed within a particular historical moment. The fact that you call your maisonette 'The Haven' and have strictly gay Christmas parties, work with or make money out of other gay people, leave your money to your 'life partner' or to Gay Switchboard, will not radically change the way that gays are portrayed on your television or the attitudes which adoption agencies would take to your application to increase the size of your family.

Well, you may say, 'It's best to keep it quiet, just go out

with friends in the evening, after all, it's my private life, no one else has to know.' This is probably the attitude of the majority of people with same-sex interests. They do not extend these to what could be labelled a *gay lifestyle*, but maintain their interests on the level of a private identity. This is one choice you may make – if you are married and wish a heterosexual identity/lifestyle to be your major interest, occasional sexual and social contact may be all the time you can spare for 'gay life'. The secrecy can continue, in the separation of this identity from the rest of your life, and problems may only arise, as in the experience of the young man related on page 90, if you are found out. The legal discrimination relating to age and public gatherings of gay people is a hazard that even the people who are keeping their homosexual contacts on a very limited basis must face. Social problems also exist in terms of risks of blackmail, and the stigma, and often violence, which are encountered by people who have same-sex interests, but wish to keep them quiet.

There is no need for people to feel themselves 'destined' to have to make a lifelong commitment or to devote themselves twenty-four hours a day to being gay. However, people who choose to keep it separate have to understand that some of the rewards of group support will not be available to counteract the stigma still attached to such interests. For those who have public heterosexual lifestyles, the problem is that their identity will seem to them in some sense 'false'. They will be playing it straight at home, at work, and everywhere except when they are socializing with gays.

In discussing the need to achieve a minimum same-sex identity, I am implying that although it is possible to achieve a personally comfortable feeling about your identity as gay and restrict its social expression, some commitment *is* necessary. In deciding how much, people have to weigh up for themselves the social costs of living more open lives (which for some people in certain jobs can be high) against the personal load you put on yourself by 'acting a lie'. For many people, a compromise position – sometimes being out, sometimes in the closet, sometimes visiting the gay scene, having casual sex, long-term friends and lovers – is worked out.

Such adjustments do not have to be permanent. Choices come – and go – with wider events in society, for example, trade union campaigns for gay rights at work, changes in the age of consent are *public* events which will affect the ways people manage their 'private' lives.

Describing someone as 'a homosexual' has no meaning. It describes no one. We need in future to look at the lifestyles of individuals who have significant same-sex interests, and these will be as varied, trouble-free, problematic, creative or restricting as those who have not developed same-sex interests. The only difference is that people with homosexual interests can never, in this society, take their lifestyles for granted. Perhaps the future trends are pointing to a culture where 'heterosexuals' may be in a similar position.

Gay signposts

London Gay Switchboard: (Tel. 01-837 7324) Available 24 hours a day.
BM Switchboard, London WC1N 3XX.

Lesbian Line: (Tel. 01-837 8602) Monday and Friday 2 p.m.–10 p.m., Tuesday–Thursday 7 p.m.–10 p.m.

Information and Advice for Women: BM Box 1514, London WC1N 3XX.

Gay Legal Problems: GLAD (Tel. 01–821 7672) 7 p.m.–10 p.m.
BM GLAD, London WC1N 3XX.

Gay News: 113/117 Farringdon Road, London EC1R 3DQ (published fortnightly).

References

1. KINSEY, A., POMEROY, W., MARTIN, C., and GEBHARD, P. (1953): *Sexual Behaviour in the Human Female*, Saunders, Philadelphia; KINSEY, A., POMEROY, W., and MARTIN, C. (1948): *Sexual Behaviour in the Human Male*, Saunders, Philadelphia; and GEBHARD, P. (1972): 'Incidence of Homosexuality in the US and Western Europe', in LIVINGOOD, J. M. (ed), *N.I.M.H. Task Force on Homosexuality: Final Report and Background Papers*, D.H.E.W. Publication No. (HSM) 72-9116, Rockville, M.D. National Institute of Mental Health.
2. BELL, A. P., and WEINBERG, M. S. (1978): *Homosexualities: A Study of Diversity Among Men and Women*, Mitchell Beazley, London.
3. MASTERS, W. H., and JOHNSON, V. E. (1979): *Homosexuality in Perspective*, Little, Brown & Co., Boston.

   Note that their claims in helping people who are 'dissatisfied' with a homosexual orientation to achieve heterosexuality should be approached cautiously in view of the special group who made up their 'sample'. Also, how 'homosexual' were they? There were additional problems in the number of people who were lost in the follow-up. In summary, we are left with the assertions of Masters and Johnson which have to be scrutinized for replicability and validity in less specialized contexts. See the review of their book by John C. Gonsiorek in *Journal of Homosexuality*, Vol. 6, No. 3, Spring 1981, Howarth Press, New York.
4. HART, J., and RICHARDSON, D. (1981): *The Theory and Practice of Homosexuality*, Routledge & Kegan Paul, London.
5. DEARDEN, H. (1929): *The Science of Happiness*, Heinemann, London.
6. MASTERS and JOHNSON, op. cit.
7. See ROWAN, R. L., and GILLETTE, P. J. (1978): *The Gay*

Health Guide, Little, Brown & Co., Boston. Also HARRIS, B., and SISLEY, E. (1977): *The Joy of Lesbian Sex*, Simon & Schuster, New York; ZILBERGELD, B. (1980): *Men and Sex,* Fontana, Glasgow (very heterosexually orientated, but good on techniques); SILVERSTEIN, C., and WHITE, E. (1977): *The Joy of Gay Sex*, Simon & Schuster, New York (illustrations particularly good).

8. WHITE, E. (1980): *States of Desire: Travels in Gay America*, André Deutsch, London.
9. FERNBACH, D. (1981): *The Spiral Path*, Gay Men's Press, London.
10. MACDONALD, A. P. Jr (1982): 'Bisexuality: Some Comments on Research and Theory', *Journal of Homosexuality,* Vol. 6, No. 3, Spring 1981, pp. 21–35, Howarth Press, New York.
11. DE CECCO, J. P. (1982): 'Definition and Meaning of Sexual Orientation', *Journal of Homosexuality*, Vol. 6, No. 4, Summer 1981, pp. 51–67.
12. MACDONALD, op. cit.
13. BELL and WEINBERG, op. cit.
14. See HARRIS and SISLEY, op. cit.; MEULENBELT, A., JOHANNA'S DAUGHTER, AMSBERG, A., LEENHOUT, S. J., and BIJMAN, S. (1981): *For Ourselves*, Sheba Feminist Publishers, London; WALKER, M. (1977): *Men Loving Men*, Gay Sunshine Press, San Francisco; SILVERSTEIN and WHITE, op. cit.
15. BIEBER, I., DAIN, H. J., DINCE, P. R., DRELLICH, M. G., GRAND, H. G., GUNDLACH, R. H., KREMAR, M. W., RIFKIN, A. H., WILBUR, C. B., and BIEBER, T. B. (1962): *Homosexuality: A Psychoanalytic Study*, Basic Books, New York.
16. MOBERLEY, E. R. (1983): *Psychogenesis: The Early Development of Gender Identity*, Routledge & Kegan Paul, London.
17. GONSIOREK, J. C. (1982): 'Results of Psychological Testing on Homosexual Populations', *American Behavioural Scientist*, Vol. 25, No. 4, March/April, pp. 385–96.
18. RUSE, M. (1982): 'Are There Gay Genes? Sociobiology and Homosexuality', *Journal of Homosexuality*, Vol. 6, No. 4, Summer 1981, pp. 5–34.

19. SPADA, J. (1979): *The Spada Report*, Signet Books, New American Library, New York.
20. MACQUARRIE, J. (1973): *Existentialism*, Penguin, Harmondsworth.
21. COHEN, S., GREEN, S., MERRYFINCH, L., JONES, G., SLADE, J., and WALKER, M. (1977): *The Law and Sexuality: How to Cope with the Law if You're Not 100% Conventionally Heterosexual*, Grass Roots Books and Manchester Law Centre, Manchester.
22. GOLUMBOK, S., SPENCER, A., and RUTTER, M. (1983): 'Children in Lesbian and Single Parent Households: Psychosexual and Psychiatric Appraisal', *Journal of Child Psychology and Psychiatry*, Vol. 24, No. 4, pp. 551–72.
23. REVOLUTIONARY GAY MEN'S CAUCUS: *The Myth of Homophobia, Reformism and Gay Liberation*, final draft 16 May 1982, RGC, 52 Acre Lane, London SW2.
24. WEEKS, J. (1981): *Sex, Politics and Society. The Regulation of Sexuality Since 1800*, Longman, London and New York.
25. PLUMMER, K. (1981): 'The Paedophile's Progress', in *Perspectives on Paedophilia*, Taylor, B. (ed.), Batsford, London.
26. WEEKS, op. cit.
27. WEST, D. J. (1960): *Homosexuality*, Pelican, Harmondsworth.
28. POLICY ADVISORY COMMITTEE ON SEXUAL OFFENCES, LONDON, HMSO: *Working Paper on the Age of Consent in Relation to Sexual Offences*, June 1979. The majority of this group recommended that the age of consent for male homosexuals be reduced to 18.
29. COLEMAN, E. (1982): 'Developmental Stages of the Coming Out Process', *American Behavioural Scientist*, Vol. 25, No. 4, March/April (pp. 469–82).

MORE ABOUT PENGUINS, PELICANS AND PUFFINS

For further information about books available from Penguins please write to Dept EP, Penguin Books Ltd, Harmondsworth, Middlesex UB7 ODA.

In the U.S.A.: For a complete list of books available from Penguins in the United States write to Dept DG, Penguin Books, 299 Murray Hill Parkway, East Rutherford, New Jersey 07073.

In Canada: For a complete list of books available from Penguins in Canada write to Penguin Books Canada Ltd, 2801 John Street, Markham, Ontario L3R IB4.

In Australia: For a complete list of books available from Penguins in Australia write to the Marketing Department, Penguin Books Australia Ltd, P.O. Box 257, Ringwood, Victoria 3134.

In New Zealand: For a complete list of books available from Penguins in New Zealand write to the Marketing Department, Penguin Books (N.Z.) Ltd, P.O. Box 4019, Auckland 10.

In India: For a complete list of books available from Penguins in India write to Penguin Overseas Ltd, 706 Eros Apartments, 56 Nehru Place, New Delhi 110019.

Published by Penguins

OUR BODIES OURSELVES

A HEALTH BOOK BY AND FOR WOMEN

Boston Women's Health Book Collective

British Edition by Angela Phillips and Jill Rakusen

The most successful book about women ever published, *Our Bodies Ourselves* has sold over one million copies worldwide.

'Every woman in the country should be issued with a copy free of charge' – *Mother and Baby*

'Well researched, informative and educational for both men and women' – *British Medical Journal*

'The Bible of the woman's health movement' – *Guardian*

'If there's only one book you ever buy – this should be it' – *19*

TREAT YOURSELF TO SEX

A GUIDE TO GOOD LOVING

Paul Brown and Carolyn Faulder

Basic, readable, sympathetic, this handbook deals with a range of sexual problems that are more common than generally supposed, and gives a series of exercises, 'sexpieces', worked out after extensive research, which, if followed honestly and carefully, will help provide workable solutions.

'By carefully following them (sexpieces), people can learn to understand their own sexuality, as well as their partner's, to their mutual advantage and pleasure' – Marje Proops

'Elegantly written digest of current sexual counselling practice . . . avoiding coyness and genteelism' – *Pulse*

Published by Penguins

THE PENGUIN BOOK OF HOMOSEXUAL VERSE

Edited by Stephen Coote

'This is a collection of poems by and about gay people. It ranges in time and place from classical Athens to contemporary New York. It ranges in tone and content from celebration to satire. While the collection can, I hope, be read for pleasure, I would like to think of it also as a record, a history of the different ways in which homosexual people have been seen and have seen themselves. Only if we know something about the past is there a chance we can do something about the future. To that extent, I would like to think of the voices collected here as those of encouragement' – Stephen Coote

The Penguin Book of Homosexual Verse includes poems from Sappho, Theocritus, Horace, Virgil, Michelangelo, and Shakespeare as well as Goethe, Byron, Verlaine, Whitman, Swinburne, Symmonds, Auden and Isherwood and many others.

WELL BEING

We over-indulge in eating and drinking, consuming the wrong kind of food in our diet; we exercise too little – or too much!; we allow the intense pressures of work and family to overwhelm us; in short, we do our best to destroy and abuse our bodies.

Based on the television series with the advice and support of the Royal College of General Practitioners, WELL BEING explores how we can take sensible and informed measures to look after ourselves. From diet and exercise, the hazards of drugs, smoking and alcohol, the diseases of modern civilization, pregnancy and childbirth, to the state of medicine today and alternative methods available, the emphasis is on encouraging us to take control of our health, fitness and well being.